PIANO CHORDS

A KEYBOARD STICKER BOOK

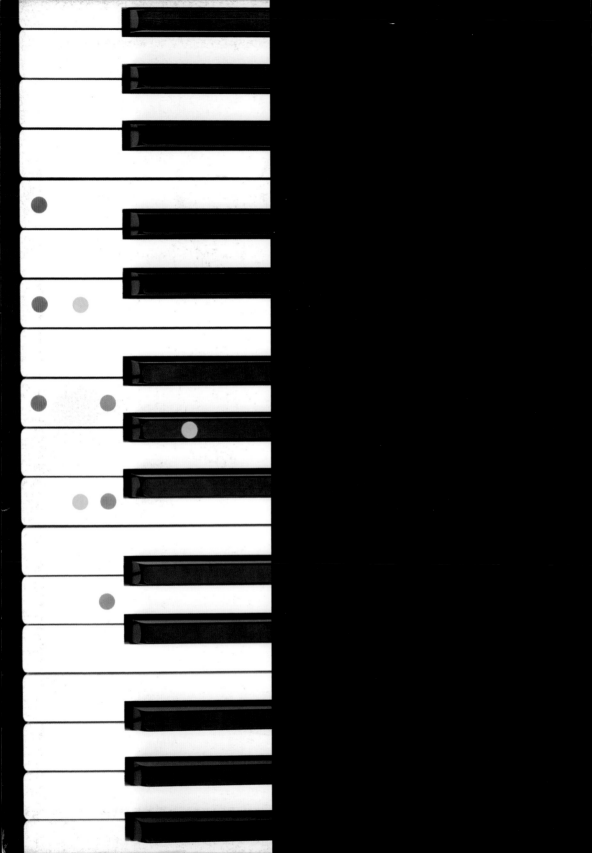

PIANO CHORDS
A KEYBOARD STICKER BOOK

HEREWARD KAYE

THUNDER BAY
P · R · E · S · S
San Diego, CA

Thunder Bay Press
An imprint of Printers Row Publishing Group
10350 Barnes Canyon Road, Suite 100, San Diego, CA 92121
www.thunderbaybooks.com

Printers Row Publishing Group is a division of Readerlink
Distribution Services, LLC. The Thunder Bay Press name and
logo are registered trademarks of Readerlink Distribution
Services, LLC.

All notations of errors or omissions should be addressed
to Thunder Bay Press, Editorial Department, at the above
address. All other correspondence (author inquiries,
permissions) concerning the content of this book should be
addressed to Quintet Publishing at the address below.

This book was conceived, designed, and produced by
The Bright Press, an imprint of The Quarto Group
The Old Brewery
6 Blundell Street
London, N7 9BH
United Kingdom
T (0)20 7700 6700 F (0)20 7700 8066
www.quartoknows.com

QTT.CHORD2

Thunder Bay Team:
Publisher: Peter Norton
Associate Publisher: Ana Parker
Publishing/Editorial Team: April Farr, Kelly Larsen,
Kathryn C. Dalby
Editorial Team: JoAnn Padgett, Melinda Allman, Traci Douglas

Quintet Publishing Team:
Managing Editor: **Rica Dearman**
Designer: **Paul Sloman** I +SUBTRACT
Photographer: **Neal Grundy**
Model: **Melissa Harrison**
Professional Musician: **Ian Radcliffe** I shineonband.co.uk
Senior Editor: **Caroline Elliker**
Editorial Director: **Emma Bastow**
Publisher: **Mark Searle**

ISBN: 978-1-68412-552-4

CONTENTS

Preface 6

Introduction 7

Level One: Macca 16

Level Two: Gaga 36

Level Three: Berlin 70

Level Four: Jools 102

Level Five: Keys 134

Glossary 176

Index 178

Acknowledgments/Credits 180

PREFACE

I was completely turned off by music at the age of eight when I was forced to take formal piano lessons for a year, but I was electrified by it at the age of ten when I saw The Beatles, live. All those incredible songs were penned by two musicians, John Lennon and Paul McCartney, who played by ear—and from then on, so did I. I have a decent musical ear—and I bet you have, too.

I found my own way around the keyboard, and it has been something of a personal mission of mine to pass on all those self-taught lessons, shortcuts, and tricks of the trade to similar aspiring musicians. For, much as musical notation has my utmost respect, is not playing by ear the zeitgeist—the feeling of our time?

In this book, you don't have to learn to read music—essential musical theory is kept to a minimum. Musical notation has been around for centuries, but we live in an age of instant communication, with so many available ways to assimilate information. So, if you want to be able to play your favorite songs on the piano or keyboard, or find your way around it to compose your own compositions, look no further.

This book is divided into five levels, from elementary to really rather good. It has a pop/rock sensibility and is built upon a foundation of illustrated chords. Helpful, peelable stickers are included to mark out specific keys involved in each chord and scale. The foundations laid down in the first two levels will enable you to predict the chords you hear in a song. It all starts with knowing your scales. From there, all the mysteries of the musical universe unravel. The scale is the DNA—all will be revealed within these pages!

Hereward Kaye

INTRODUCTION:

Once upon a time, I had a musical, *Moby Dick*, that made it into London's West End. This was in large part due to the skills of our musical arranger, Martin Koch. He told me his grandmother had taught him to play the piano at the age of three, with the aid of brightly colored stickers. Martin went on to become the conductor of *Les Misérables*, arranged *Mamma Mia!* for Björn and Benny from Abba, and arranged *Billy Elliot* for Elton John. So, if you're a piano beginner, whatever your age, stickers are the way forward.

The aim of this book is to teach you how to learn all your favorite songs as quickly and coherently as possible, with the aid of handy stickers that you'll find at the back of the book. However, there are a few things you need to know before we begin.

UP AND DOWN

When this book says up, it means to the right, as you face the keyboard, in the direction of the higher notes. When this book says down, it means to the left, as you face the keyboard, in the direction of the lower notes.

TONES AND SEMITONES

A semitone (also known as a half step) is the shortest distance you can travel on the keyboard. Two semitones add up to a tone (also known as a whole step). On the illustration below, you'll see that the distance traveled from the white note of C to the white note of D is a tone. This is because there is another note between the two—a black note. From E to F however is a semitone, because there is no other (black) note between them.

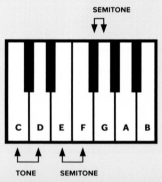

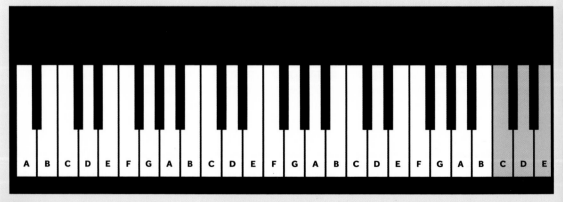

BLACK NOTES (SHARPS AND FLATS)

Each black note has a sharp name and a flat name. It is sharp of the note immediately before it, and flat of the note immediately after it. In formal musical notation, the note's name is determined by the key. But it is not my intention to blind you with musical science. This book is dedicated to getting you up and running as directly as possible. Therefore, we will simply refer to the black notes as sharps when traveling in an upward direction, and flats when traveling in a downward direction, until you get deeper into the book.

This is the symbol for a sharp: #
This is the symbol for a flat: ♭

OCTAVES

An octave is the distance traveled from one note to when that same note is next encountered further up the keyboard. It is a sequence of twelve (semitone) notes until, on playing the thirteenth note, we find we are playing the same note we started with, only higher in pitch—one octave, to be exact.

A full-length keyboard has seven octaves in a row. You may be learning to play on a shorter-length keyboard, with four or five octaves, but no matter. Once you've learned what goes on within a single octave, you've learned everything. The magic happens within those twelve notes. After that, you just repeat yourself, upward or downward in pitch, in however many octaves march along your keyboard.

Before you dive into the book, notice the names of the blue notes on the diagram below. This is an octave, from C to C. It's alphabetical, up to and including G. Then it starts again from A. So those notes are C, D, E, F, G, A, B, C.

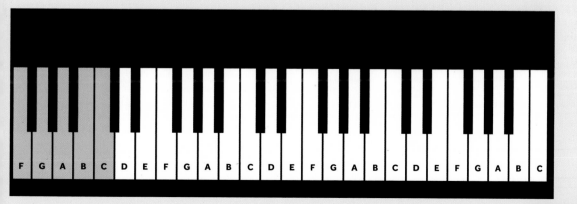

CHORD SHAPES

A chord happens when we strike three or more keys at the same time to make a harmonious sound. To begin with, our chords will be grouped into recognizable shapes. Later on, they will be grouped into chord "families."

Almost all the chords in this book are made up of three notes and played with the right hand. The diagrams of chords in this book give you the names of those three individual notes involved in the chord you are learning.

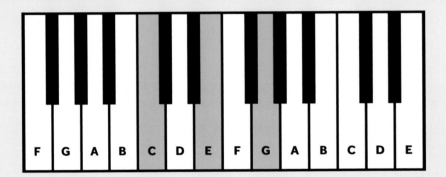

USING THE STICKERS

There are hundreds of stickers at the back of this book, in a variety of colors. They are reusable and easy to stick onto a key and remove or move when no longer needed there.

These stickers will be vital in the early days of learning chords, as they will help you to locate chords quickly and easily, so you'll know exactly where to position your fingers. You could assign different colors to different chord groups and scales.

When marking up more than one chord at a time, you may find that two or more stickers are needed on the same piano key. Don't worry—there's plenty of room to accommodate several stickers. You may also find that it will be useful to write down the name of the note upon the sticker—or you could write down which finger to use for that key.

As you progress through the book, you'll get to the level where you may not need the stickers to memorize chords and scales. But as you advance further, remember that they are there, should you wish to utilize them.

STEP-BY-STEP

Take a look at the example chords in the diagrams below.

* The stickers in **diagram a** show one chord (C Major). To apply the stickers, simply drop them onto a key and press down firmly. When you want to remove them, simply use your fingernail to peel them off the keys—the adhesive is gentle enough to leave no residue.

* Two chords share the same finger position, twice, in **diagram b**. The stickers are small enough to fit onto each of these keys.

* In **diagram c**, the pianist's fingers are able to locate the chords easily, by pressing on keys containing the same-colored stickers.

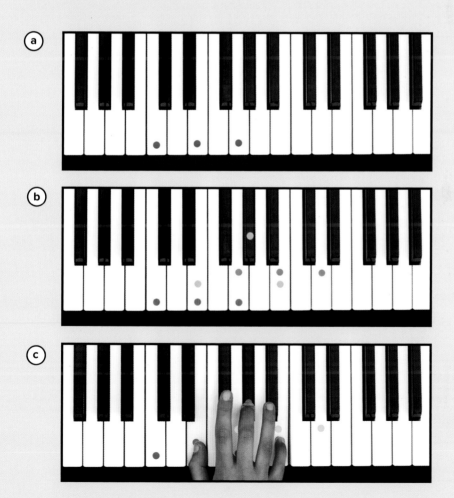

RIGHT HAND, LEFT HAND

In this book, you will be playing single notes with your left hand and chords with your right. It doesn't make any difference whether you're left-handed or right-handed.

When referring to the fingers on your hand, we will call your thumb "finger 1," your index finger "finger 2," your middle finger is "finger 3," the one next to it "finger 4," and your little finger "finger 5."

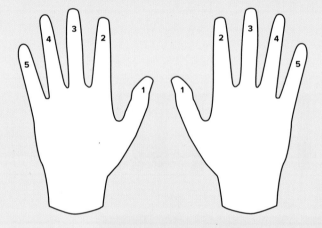

PIANO VERSUS KEYBOARD

A keyboard may be less expensive than an acoustic piano; it can also connect to a computer for music-production software; and it allows headphones to be plugged in, so the learner can practice without disturbing others. However, an acoustic piano produces sound from real strings on wood. Ensure yours is in tune and that the keys are in good working order.

PEDALS

Old-fashioned, upright acoustic pianos usually have two pedals: the left is a soft pedal, which softens the sound when pressed. The right is a sustain pedal, which keeps the note ringing when pressed. Most modern and grand pianos have three pedals; the third is a "damper"—when pressed, it stops the note ringing.

Electronic keyboards usually have a pedal that you can plug into either a sustain or damper socket. Go for the sustain option. Whenever you play a chord that needs to ring out, keep your foot down on the sustain pedal, but lift it when you change chord. You don't want the notes of one chord sustaining through to the following chord, as the combination of both usually results in a rather unharmonious discord.

KEYBOARD SOUNDS

A keyboard comes with a selection of different sounds, not just the piano sound. These vary according to cost of the keyboard you have bought, or the era that keyboard comes from (when they were all called "synthesizers"— there are classic synths from previous decades that define the sound of many of the records from each era).

However basic, typically, your keyboard will have at least these four sounds: piano, strings, electric piano and organ. Choose the one you want and proceed to play just as you would with a piano.

HAND POSITIONING

Keep your hand arched so your fingertips are pressing on the keys as you play. Imagine you have a mouse on the keyboard—it should be able to run under the tunnel of your hand!

When learning to play the chords in this book, keep your wrists relaxed, as in the images below. Some chords might be difficult to play, but do try different hand positions if they feel more comfortable.

HOW TO USE THIS BOOK

The five sections in this book may look like chapters, but they're levels that you progress through as you learn more about playing piano/keyboards. If you have some experience already, flick through the book until you find your entry level and proceed from there.

Each of these sections are named after well-known, inspiring piano players who have composed, upon the instrument you are about to learn, some of the many great tunes that form the soundtrack of our lives. We start with some of the most basic chords that get progressively more difficult as you move through the book. Along the way you'll find helpful diagrams, illustrations, and photographs that show you exactly where on the keyboard to place your fingers. Chord sequences then enable you to piece together and play musical compositions.

GLOSSARY

As you work your way through the book, you'll come across some technical terms you may not know. Refer to the glossary on page 176, which gives a quick definition of these terms.

LEVEL ONE: MACCA

Paul McCartney lends his name to our beginner level here, though this in no way disparages the magnificence of his music. Rather, it reflects the fact that he wrote many of his great songs on the piano without being able to read a note of music. But he worked it out, with a little help from his friends, and created some of the classic songs of the twentieth century. I once heard him teach a master class that gave the eager piano beginner their first six chords in double-quick time. So, that's where we're going to start.

MIDDLE C

First, we're going to locate middle C.

You'll see there is a group of three black keys bunched together, and a group of two. For now, use these two groups of black keys as markers to help you find your way around.

Round about the middle of your keyboard, locate the white key immediately before the two black keys.

Put a sticker on it—perhaps a red one.

YOUR FIRST CHORD: C Major

With your right hand, rest finger 1 on the white note on which you have just placed a sticker: middle C. Skip the white note next to it, and put finger 3 on the note after that. Skip the white note next to it, and put finger 5 on the note after that.

You now have three fingers on three notes. Press them down together. That's C Major, your first chord, made up of three individual notes: C, E, and G.

Put red stickers on the two new notes, so that the chord of C Major is clearly marked up, as in the images below. Take note of the shape: three white notes, with a white note separating each of them. This is shape one.

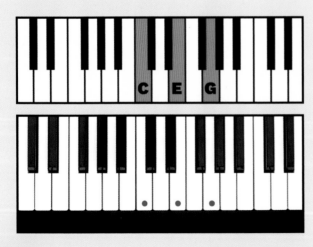

FIVE MORE SHAPE-ONE CHORDS

D minor, E minor, F Major, G Major, A minor

Rest your appropriate fingers on the three notes with stickers so that you are in the C Major position. Keeping the same shape, move up the keyboard (to the right) by one white note. So, it's just like C Major, but one note further along. This is D minor, which is written like this: D^m.

D^m

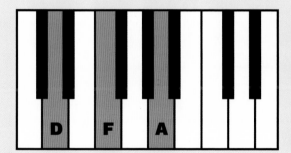 

E^m

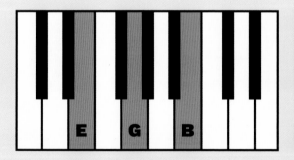 

Again, keeping the same shape, move one more note along. This is E minor, which is written like this: E^m.

Move the same shape-one white note further up and it becomes F Major.

Although your minor chords will always have a small m beside the capital letter to denote its minor status, with Major chords, we usually dispense with the word Major—this chord is written simply as F.

F Major

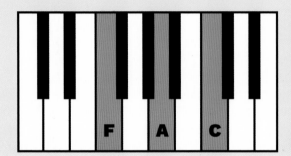 

G Major

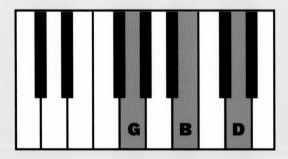 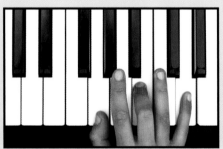

Move the same shape up another note, and it becomes G Major, or G.

A minor

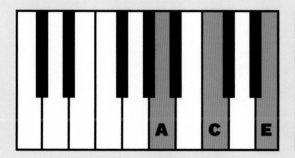 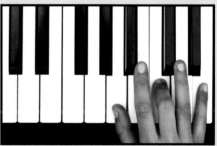

Move the same shape up another note, and it becomes A minor, or A^m.

There you have your six shape-one chords. Turn the page to find out how you're going to play them in sequence.

It's been covered by Stevie Wonder, Tina Turner, Tom Jones, and Al Green. But Bill Withers didn't even make his first recording until he was thirty-two. With royalties, he bought a little keyboard and with the shape of C, ran his hand up and down the keyboard without altering the shape, as you have just done. The words "lean on me" came into his head, he said, because he came from a rural background where people looked after each other.

PRACTICE WHAT YOU'VE LEARNED

The tune of the Bill Withers classic "Lean on Me" works well with the chords you have just learned. Have a go at playing it with these same chords.

Try this. Sing the three words of the first line, then hit the chord:

C

On the next four words, play your C chord again, with the first word, then move the shape up one white note, as you have just learned, with every next word. Each time you move it, the name of the chord changes. Do this very slowly:

C   D^m E^m F

For the next four words, play those same chords in reverse, coming back down the keyboard:

F   E^m D^m C

Then play one chord per word for the last line, upward from C to E^m (which you play for two words in succession), before coming back down one chord to D^m for the last word:

C   D^m E^m E^m D^m

COUNTING TIME

Now you need to learn how to count the beats of a bar.

What's a bar? A short measure of music, the length of which is determined by its time signature. What's a time signature? It's like this:

MUSICAL NOTATION—4/4 TIME SIGNATURE

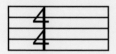

It looks like a fraction, doesn't it? In musical notation it appears at the beginning of a piece of music. The top figure of the two is the one to take note of. This time signature tells us the song is in "four four." In other words, there are four beats in the bar.

SHAPE ONE, CHORD SEQUENCE ONE

Position finger 1, finger 3, and finger 5 on the three stickers you marked up earlier, ready for the first chord: C. Count to four at the speed of four tick-tocks of a clock—nice and slowly. Then play the C chord on the first beat of the next bar. Keep counting the four beats of each bar aloud at the same steady pace and move on to the next chord for the restart of the next bar.

You are going to strike each next chord as you say number one. Be careful to keep your hand in the same shape-one configuration, and gradually move up the keyboard with it, as each new chord comes along at the start of each new bar. Like this:

1	2	3	4		1	2	3	4		1	2	3	4		1	2	3	4
Count				-	C				-	Dᵐ				-	Eᵐ			

1	2	3	4		1	2	3	4		1	2	3	4
F				-	G				-	Aᵐ			

ARPEGGIATING YOUR CHORD

Do the sequence again, but this time, instead of putting all three fingers down together and playing it as a chord, try playing the individual notes one at a time—finger 1, then finger 3, then finger 5. This is known as arpeggiating your chord. Once you have done this with C, move on to D^m and do the same thing: play the chord one note at a time, from finger 1 to finger 5. Then E^m, then F, then G, then A^m.

Practice doing it while counting the four beats of the bar (nice and slowly), playing the first note on the count of one, the second note on the count of two, the third note on the count of three. On the fourth beat of the bar, move on to the next chord.

It's time to learn the names of all the notes you just played. To do that, we need to learn the scale of C Major.

SCALE OF C MAJOR

Here's the correct fingering for playing a scale: using your right hand, play the first three notes with your first three fingers—so finger 1 plays the note of C, then finger 2 plays the note of D, then finger 3 plays the note of E (as shown in **image a**, below). This leaves five notes to play and you have five fingers to play them with. So, move finger 1 to the fourth note of the scale, the F, and using your whole hand one finger after another (starting with finger 1, ending with finger 5), play **FGABC** (as shown in **image b**, below).

Try it again in one fluid movement: the first three notes from finger 1, the next five notes from finger 1 to finger 5. Now—this is more difficult—try playing it in reverse, from the top note back down to the bottom note. All five fingers, then finger 3 to finger 1 for the last three notes. The scale, played downward in this way, is actually the melody to a well-known hymn: "Joy to the world, the Lord is come."

We've started with the scale of C because it is the easiest of all the scales to play. It is white notes only. No black notes are involved, which means the scale of C has no sharps or flats. Just the letters of the alphabet from A to G, starting at C. There is no "HIJK . . ." in music—once you pass G, you start again from A.

Before you go any further, learn the names of these white notes. Since your piano/keyboard is a daisy chain of octaves, by learning the names and positions of these eight white notes, you will have learned the name of every white note on the keyboard, as the same notes are replicated all the way along.

Test yourself:
1. What is the white note immediately below the two black notes?
2. What is the white note immediately above the two black notes?
3. What is the white note immediately below the three black notes?
4. What is the white note immediately above the three black notes?

Now go back to the six shape one chords you already learned.

Test yourself:
1. What are the three notes in your chord of C Major?
2. What are the three notes in your chord of D minor?
3. What are the three notes in your chord of E minor?
4. What are the three notes in your chord of F Major?
5. What are the three notes in your chord of G Major?
6. What are the three notes in your chord of A minor?

Answers: 1. C; 2. E; 3. F; 4. B
1. C, E, G; 2. D, F, A; 3. E, G, B; 4. F, A, C; 5. G, B, D; 6. A, C, E

INTERVALS

In two places within this octave, there are two white notes next to each other, undivided by a black note. You'll see immediately after the two black notes together, we have E and F. Immediately after the three black notes, we have B and C. This is important, as we turn now to look at the intervals involved in this (and every other) scale.

An interval is the distance between two notes, measured in semitones. A semitone is the shortest distance we can travel on the keyboard, from one note to the next—the distance from one note to its immediate neighbor, definitely *not* forgetting the black notes, which are all important as we make this calculation.

Look at the first two notes: C to D. There is another note between them, a black one. So the interval between them is **2** semitones (C to the black note above it, the black note above it to the D).

The next two notes of the scale are D to E. Once again, there is another note between them, a black one. So the interval is **2** semitones.

Now we come to the first of our two white notes together: E and F. With no black note to separate them, the interval is **1** semitone.

F to G has a black note between, so **2** semitones. Same with G to A—**2** semitones. Same with A to B—there is a black note between, so **2** semitones.

Now we come to the second of our two white notes together: B and C. With no black note between, the interval is **1** semitone.

We've traveled a full octave. Now we have our sequence of intervals: **2 2 1 2 2 2 1**

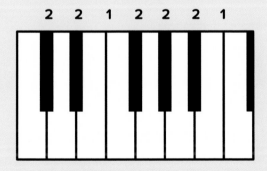

Every major scale you play will have this same sequence of intervals. Remember the number as if it were the combination to your own safe! For it will unlock many of the mysteries of musical theory.

There are other intervals within the scale.

From first note C to third note E is—as you would expect—a **third**.

From first note C to fourth note F is a **fourth** (like the first two notes of "O Little Town of Bethlehem").

From first note C to fifth note G is a **fifth** (like the first four notes of "Twinkle, Twinkle, Little Star").

And so on, with the sixth and seventh notes.

SHAPE ONE, CHORD SEQUENCE TWO

C – A^m – F – G

Move down the keyboard this time, from one chord to the next, until you get to the last one (G), when you will go up.

Count yourself in, as slowly as a ticking clock, and play the chord on the first beat of each bar. The chord lasts for the whole bar. Musicians call this "one-in-the-bar."

1	2	3	4		1	2	3	4		1	2	3	4		1	2	3	4
C				-	A^m				-	F				-	G			

Now, instead of striking the chord (all three notes at the same time), you're going to arpeggiate it (play each note individually). Playing the three notes of each chord in sequence, from bottom (finger 1) note to top (finger 5) note, you are going to play a note on each beat of the bar. As there are four beats in the bar and only three notes in a chord, you're going to play the first note of each chord *twice*. Like this:

1	2	3	4		1	2	3	4		1	2	3	4		1	2	3	4
C	C	E	G	-	A	A	C	E	-	F	F	A	C	-	G	G	B	D

Remember, the letters in this illustration refer to single notes, not chords. Keep it nice and slow, so that you have time to *stay* in time, changing from one chord to the next. When you've got the hang of it, then you can speed it up a little.

I'll bet you're thinking: "Where have I heard this before?" You're actually playing Hoagy Carmichael's 1938 song "Heart and Soul," which features in the Tom Hanks movie *Big*. Hanks' character is in a toy store that has illuminated piano keys on the floor, and he jumps from one to the other. If you've not seen this, buy the DVD!

Hoagy Carmichael is famous for his classic song "Stardust," which Paul McCartney said was the one song he wished he had written. But "Heart and Soul" has become a standard for piano beginners, rather like another piece called "Chopsticks." It's a classic chord progression, underpinning all those doo-wop songs from the 1950s and 60s.

THREE-CHORD TRICK: PRIMARY MAJORS

Every key has three Major chords belonging to it and the scale shows us how to find them. It's a simple trick that, once mastered, will give you the DNA—the building blocks—of almost every pop song ever written. Pop music grew out of the blues—classic three-chord territory. Rare indeed in the modern era is the song not built upon a foundation of these three chords.

The three chords are known as primary Majors and are built upon the first, fourth, and fifth notes of the scale. Leonard Cohen actually referred to them at the moment they occur in his brilliant song "Hallelujah": "It goes like this, the fourth, the fifth."

Here's how it's done: Find the first note of the scale. That one is easy because the scale is always named after the first note. So, in the case of the C scale, that note is C. Make a Major chord there: C Major.

Next, locate and name the fourth note of the scale and build a Major chord there. That fourth note is F and the chord, therefore, is F Major.

Now locate and name the fifth note of the scale and build a Major chord there. That fifth note is G, so the chord is G Major.

So, the three primary chords associated with the key of **C** are **C**, **F**, and **G**.

Play this sequence, two beats on each chord:

1	2	3	4		1	2	3	4		1	2	3	4		1	2	3	4
C		C		-	F		F		-	G		G		-	F		F	

It could be "Twist and Shout," "Wild Thing," or "La Bamba," and if we muck about with the order of the chords, it's practically every other pop song ever written in C. In those songs, it may be that there are a couple more chords involved, but I'm going to show you how to predict what they may be, too. Again, they can be found by applying another simple formula to the Major scale.

SIX-CHORD TRICK: RELATIVE MINORS

Let's turn those three chords into six. Every Major chord has a minor chord that belongs to it. This is known as a relative minor. Here's how you find it:

From the Major chord, **go down three semitones** on the keyboard and build a minor chord.

Apply that to each of our three primary triads (the fancy name for a chord) in C Major, to find each of their relative minors.

So, C first. From the note of C, go down three semitones. Don't include the C—start with the white note immediately below the C. We know that to be the note of B. Next down from the B is a black note (don't forget those black notes)—B flat, which is written B♭. That's the second semitone. One more to go. The semitone below the B♭ is a white note, which we know to be A. We've traveled three semitones down from the C. All we do now is make a minor chord on that note of A—the chord of A minor, which you have already met.

So the **relative minor of C Major** is **A minor**.

Try playing the C, followed by the A minor. You can hear that they belong together; they seem to fit.

Repeat the process with our next primary Major chord, the F. One semitone down is the white note right next to it, heading down the keyboard. We know it to be an E. Then there is a black note. This is E flat, written E♭. That's two semitones traveled, one to go. The white note directly one semitone down is a D. We're there. Time to build a minor chord there: D minor.

The **relative minor of F Major** is **D minor**.

Our third primary Major is G. The black note immediately before it is G flat, written G♭. The white note immediately below the G♭ is F. One more semitone to go. The white note next to the F is E. We have arrived three semitones down from the G. Build a minor chord there: E minor.

The **relative minor of G Major** is **E minor**.

And there we have our six chords that all belong to the key of C.

Try playing the six chords of the key of C in this order. A really slow count of four, then strike the first chord on the first beat of the bar, the second chord on beat three of the same bar, and so on. In other words, two different chords in each bar, two beats on each chord. Like this:

1	2	3	4		1	2	3	4		1	2	3	4		1	2	3	4
C		A^m		-	F		D^m		-	G		E^m		-	C		C	

BLACK NOTES, FLAT NAMES

Time to meet the black notes. As you are by now aware, they have both a flat name and a sharp name. For the moment, we will get to know them by their flat names.

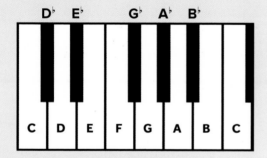

Test yourself:

1. What is the first black note in the block of two black notes?
2. What is the first black note in the block of three black notes?
3. What is the second black note in the block of two black notes?
4. What is the second black note in the block of three black notes?
5. What is the third black note in the block of three black notes?

Answers: 1. D♭; 2. G♭; 3. E♭; 4. A♭; 5. B♭

SHAPE ONE, CHORD SEQUENCE THREE

You've almost completed the first level. Here's a chord sequence that might have a familiar ring to it . . . this is the verse sequence, which plays twice:

1	2	3	4		1	2	3	4		1	2	3	4		1	2	3	4
C		C		-	G		G		-	A^m		A^m		-	F		F	

1	2	3	4		1	2	3	4		1	2	3	4		1	2	3	4
C		C		-	G		G		-	F		E^m	D^m	-	C			

Don't worry about the timing of the last bit, just go straight down through F, E^m, D^m, and C as you did with "Lean on Me."

This is the chorus of this new tune. It uses the same chords, just slightly rearranged in the first four bars, then exactly the same as the previous sequence in the home stretch:

1	2	3	4		1	2	3	4		1	2	3	4		1	2	3	4
A^m		A^m		-	E^m		E^m		-	F		F		-	C		C	

1	2	3	4		1	2	3	4		1	2	3	4		1	2	3	4
C		C		-	G		G		-	F		E^m	D^m	-	C			

It has a "bridge"—the bit in songs where the songwriter gives you a change from the repetition of the verse and chorus, to take you somewhere else. This particular bridge brings together all your chords, in descending sequence:

F   E^m   D^m   C   –   B♭   A^m   G   F   C

There is a chord of **B flat** that you haven't yet learned. Just do a chord of C one note further down and move finger 1 onto the black note, like this:

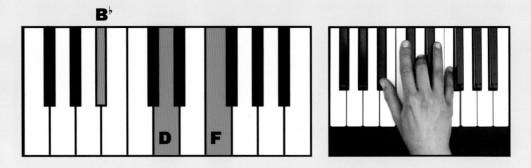

Got it? Then slot it into the chord rundown, like this:

F   E^m   D^m   C   –   B♭   A^m   G   F   C

Does the tune sound familiar? It should sound a bit like The Beatles' "Let it Be."

WELL DONE ON LEVEL ONE—YOU'RE NOW A MACCA!

John Lennon didn't like the song "Let it Be"—he thought it sounded "biblical"—but the public certainly did. "Mother Mary" referred to Paul's mother Mary, who died when he was just fourteen. She appeared to him in an anxiety dream and calmed him, which compelled him to write the song. Unbelievably, he also wrote "The Long and Winding Road" on that same day.

LEVEL TWO: GAGA

The queen of level two is a formidable pianist—an aspect of this multitalented artist that is upstaged by the outrageously provocative images she creates for herself. No one better encompasses the world of pop with a piano at its heart than Stefani Joanna Angeline Germanotta, one of the greatest-selling album artists of all time, otherwise known as Lady Gaga. In this level, you will learn more Major chords, this time involving the black notes as well.

INVERSIONS

Now you have six chords, all belonging to the key of C. We're going to turn those six chords into eighteen. Once again, all we need is a simple formula.

These six chords—and any chords for that matter—can be played in three different positions. We've learned them in one position: the root position. You know them as three Major and three minor chords, but they are Major and minor chords in the **root** position. That is, the first note in the chord, the one under finger 1, is the note after which the chord is named. In musical theory, this is known as the tonic. This chord can be "shuffled"—using the same notes, but in a different order. It has a **first inversion** and a **second inversion**.

When playing a song, it helps to be able to play a chord in a variety of different positions so that your hands aren't leaping all over the keyboard. We do this by taking the chords we already know, made up of the same three notes, and rearranging them.

Imagine the three notes of the root chord are three cards in your hand. Take the card on your left and put it on the right. Those cards are now in the equivalent position of the first inversion. Now do it again—take the card on your left and put it on the right. Those cards are now in the equivalent position of the second inversion.

Take the chord of C. You know those notes from left to right to be **C**, **E**, and **G**.

C Major

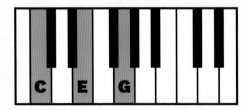

C Major: 1st inversion

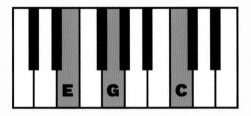 

Take the note on your left and put it on the right. How? By making a mental note of the note you are moving, the one that rests beneath finger 1 and, before you move your hand, locate it visually an octave up. That's the C. You're heading for the white note before the two black ones, one octave higher. Now move your hand across, so that finger 1 goes to the second note and the finger that was there—finger 2—goes to the third note. Finger 5 is now free to play the C you have located one octave higher. Your hand is now in the C first inversion position, and the notes from left to right read E, G, and C.

C Major: 2nd inversion

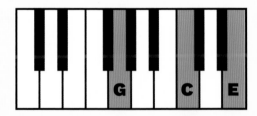 

Shuffle along once more for the second inversion (but first make sure you take a mental photo of where finger 1 is before you move it). Lose the note at the bottom, the E, and replicate it an octave higher. All finger 1 and finger 2 have to do is jump onto the next two notes you already have covered. Finger 5 heads for E, an octave up.

Once in the second inversion position, of course, one more finger shuffle along and you're back at C in the root position, but one octave higher. In this way, you can literally "walk" a chord from the bottom of your keyboard to the top.

THE LEFT HAND

As you look at your right hand, poised for action, ask yourself: "Where have I seen one of these before?" That's right, on the other side of your body! Piano playing is a two-handed game, so let the multitasking begin!

TWO-HANDED SEQUENCE

The right hand is simple indeed. It plays only two chords: **C** in its second inversion position, and a "normal" **A minor** in its root position, with minimal movement required to change one to the other.

C Major: 2nd inversion   **A minor**

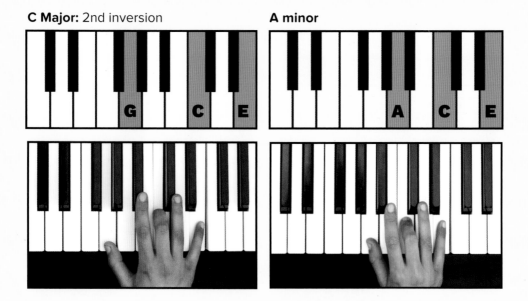

This particular example of one chord changing to another personifies why we use inversions, because to move from this inversion of **C Major** to **A minor** means we only have to change *one finger*. We really don't want to be bombing up and down the keyboard all the time—that's just going to put us out of time. The closer together the chords are, the better. So, we choose the inversions of each chord that minimize the changes from one to another, in the area of the keyboard that most suits the song and pleases the ear.

You are going to play each chord with your right hand on the first beat of the bar. There are four beats in the bar, so you are counting *one two three four*.

Similarly, your left hand will play on the first beat of the bar. But just a single note. This is the style of pop piano—chords with the right hand, single notes with the left. Most of the time, the left hand will be playing the root note of whatever chord you are playing with your other hand. So, if the three fingers on your right hand are putting down a chord of C, finger 1 (your thumb) of your left hand is simultaneously playing the *note* of C.

As I say, most of the time—but not always! That root note emphatically emphasizes the chord, no doubt about it, but there are two other notes available. Think about it. Your right hand is playing a chord—three notes in mellifluous conjunction. Which means, if any of those three notes were to be picked out in the left hand, it's going to work with the chord.

This sequence demonstrates the point. Here's the right hand on its own. Remember, you are playing the second inversion of C, with finger 1 on the note of G, finger 3 on C, and finger 5 on E. When the chord changes, all you need to do is move finger 1 up one white note to change the chord to an A minor.

RIGHT HAND (chords)

1	2	3	4		1	2	3	4		1	2	3	4		1	2	3	4
C 2nd				-	C 2nd				-	Aᵐ				-	Aᵐ			

With the left hand, you'll play C, then E, followed by F—a note that isn't one of the three notes in the chord at all. What the left-hand note does here is change the A minor into a different chord entirely—in this case, an F Major 7th, a chord you will encounter later in the book.

LEFT HAND (single notes)

1	2	3	4		1	2	3	4		1	2	3	4		1	2	3	4
C				-	E				-	F				-	F			

Put them together and magic happens!

	1	2	3	4		1	2	3	4		1	2	3	4		1	2	3	4
Right	C ^{2nd}				-	C ^{2nd}				-	A^m				-	A^m			
Left	C				-	E				-	F				-	F			

Listen to the way the first chord of C, playing to its own namesake in the left hand, becomes transformed when, in the second bar, the left hand plays an E. In the third and fourth bar, the note of F changes the right-hand chord of A^m into something else entirely, but that's an explanation for another day.

That's the first half of the sequence. Play it twice in a row, followed by this second half to the sequence, which also needs playing twice:

	1	2	3	4		1	2	3	4		1	2	3	4		1	2	3	4
Right	A^m				-	C ^{2nd}				-	A^m				-	A^m			
Left	A				-	C				-	F				-	F			

The two-handed sequence you have just played fits perfectly with "Use Somebody" by Kings of Leon. Give it a listen, then try the chords again, playing along with the track, to see how similar it sounds.

Brothers Caleb and Jared named their band Kings of Leon after their grandfather. "Use Somebody" was written by Caleb, who found the sound, groove, and chord sequence by speeding up Joe Cocker and Jennifer Warnes' "Up Where We Belong." So now you've got two numbers you can play along to.

MUSICAL NOTATION: THE TREBLE CLEF STAVE

E   F   G   A   B   C   D   E   F

This is a musical stave. The symbol at the beginning of it is known as a **treble clef**. It represents the notes above middle C on your keyboard. There won't be a great deal of "old-school" musical notation in this book, but there will be some, to demystify the everyday tools of the "reading" musician and give you a basic working knowledge.

A note is represented by a blob either on or in between the lines of the stave. You'll see there are five lines and four spaces.

The notes assigned to the *lines* from bottom to top are: **E G B D F**. It is usually—and easily—remembered by the acronym **E**very **G**ood **B**oy **D**eserves **F**ootball. These are shown in blue in the illustration above.

The notes assigned to the *spaces* from bottom to top are: **F A C E**. This one couldn't be easier to commit to memory, as it spells the word "face." These are shown in pink in the illustration above.

However, sometimes notes fall above or below the five lines of the treble clef's stave, as is the case with the C Major scale, which we're going to notate now. Usually in manuscripted pieces of piano music we have two staves, one on top of the other—the treble clef stave on top, and the bass clef stave underneath.

Middle C actually falls midway between the two. We deal with it by using a "ledger line"—a short line running through the note in question.

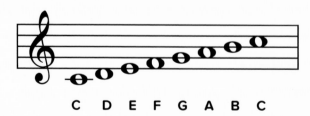

C   D   E   F   G   A   B   C

MUSICAL NOTATION: THE BASS CLEF STAVE

G   A   B   C   D   E   F   G   A

This musical stave represents a lower range of keys—the keys below middle C—typically covered by your left hand. There are five lines and four spaces.

The notes assigned to the *lines* from bottom to top are: **G B D F A**. Use the acronym **G**ood **B**oys **D**eserve **F**ootball **A**lways. These are shown in blue in the illustration above.

The notes assigned to the *spaces* from bottom to top are: **A C E G**. Your handy acronym? **A**ll **C**ows **E**at **G**rass. These are shown in pink in the illustration above.

If you carry on up from the top "A" line, the space immediately above it will be B, and the imaginary line above it will be C. Not any old C—it's middle C; like treble clef and bass clef tunnel workers digging from each end, you've met in the middle. This now becomes apparent as we put the two staves one above the other, in their typical arrangement:

BOTH STAVES: DOUBLE C MAJOR SCALE

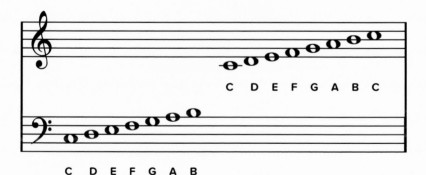

C   D   E   F   G   A   B   C

C   D   E   F   G   A   B

MORE CHORD SHAPES

In the last level you learned six shape-one chords, which turned into eighteen when you found how to reposition them as inversions. Here, we are going to meet three more chord shapes, each involving three Major chords. These nine chords will then become twenty-seven when going through the inversion process. From here on in, the chords and scales you are introduced to will involve a combination of white notes and black notes.

BLACK NOTES, SHARP NAMES

The black notes will be referred to as either flats or sharps, depending on the circumstances. You know them by their flat names already (see page 32), so you should now acquaint yourself with the black notes by their "sharp names."

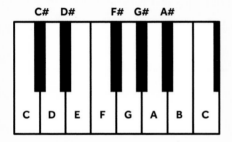

It can be confusing, knowing when to refer to black notes as sharps or flats. For the purposes of this book, I will generally call them sharps when our activity takes us up the keyboard, and flats when our activity takes us down the keyboard. However, when you're doing scales, I will refer to them by the correct name for that particular scale. By the end of this level, you will understand why they are so-called.

SHAPE TWO CHORDS: A D E

Here is the chord of A Major. Think of this shape as a triangle, pointing upward, like a steeple. There is a black note in the middle, and white notes on either side.

....

A Major

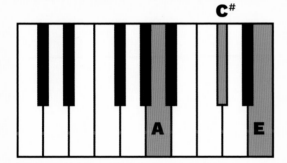

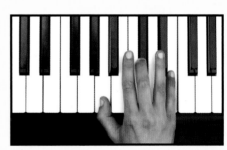

Two other chords share the same shape:

....

D Major

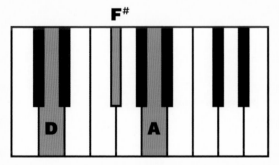

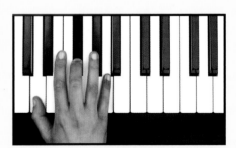

E Major

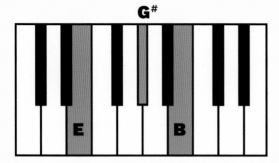

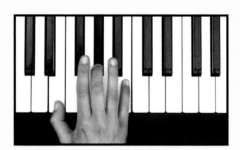

SHAPE TWO: CHORD SEQUENCE

In this sequence, you are going to strike the chord three times per bar—on each of the first three beats of the bar. On the fourth beat you are going to move to the next chord, in time for the first beat of the following bar.

On the first beat of each bar in this sequence, as well as striking the chord with the fingers of your right hand, you are going to play the root note of the chord one octave further down, with finger 1 of your left hand. "Which one's the root note?" you ask. It's the note the chord is named after. Finger 1 of the right hand is on it. So, check that note out and locate it one octave down, for finger 1 on your left hand. When you play it, keep it pressed down for the duration of the bar—just one "strike" while your right hand strikes the chord three times. With the right hand, on the last bar, end with a single chord, to finish it off nicely.

The back of this book is loaded with stickers, so make use of them here. Place three stickers on the three notes your left hand needs to play, to locate them instantly.

	1	2	3	4		1	2	3	4		1	2	3	4		1	2	3	4
Right	A	A	A		-	D	D	D		-	E	E	E		-	A			
Left	A				-	D				-	E				-	A			

SHAPE TWO: INVERSIONS

Earlier, you learned how to put your chord through inversions, which involved rearranging the three notes involved, like three cards in your hand. Each time, you removed the lowest of the three notes in your chord and reproduced it an octave up (like taking the card on the left-hand side and putting it on the right). Playing-wise, you achieved this by shuffling your fingers along.

Let's now apply that process to your shape-two chords.

A MAJOR, ROOT, 1ST, AND 2ND INVERSION

Here is A in its three positions. First, the "root," which you have already met, with notes (from left to right) A, C#, E:

....

A Major: root

Note that the left hand plays the root note of A here.

A Major: 1st inversion

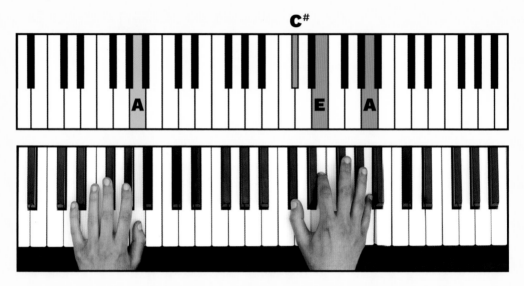

Now take finger 1 off the A. Shuffle it along to the next note in the chord, C#. Take finger 2 off C# and shuffle it along to the next note in the chord, E. Move finger 5 up to the note of A.

A Major: 2nd inversion

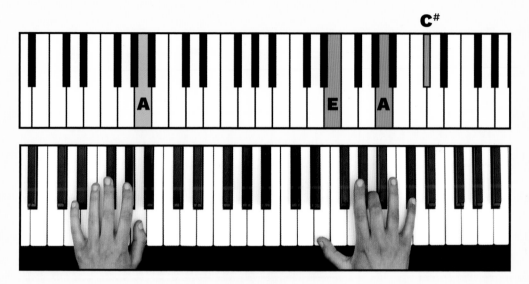

Shuffle along once more—lose the note at the bottom, the C#, and replicate it an octave higher. All finger 1 and finger 3 have to do is jump onto the next two notes you already have covered, as finger 5 heads for the C#.

Did you notice the pattern of moving the chords up the keyboard as you travel from the root position to the first inversion and then the second inversion positions?

Now try the root and both inversions of D and E. The diagrams on the following pages show how your right hand progresses up the keyboard as you play these notes. Keep finger 1 of your left hand on the root note, at least one octave down, as the right hand plays the chords.

D MAJOR, ROOT, 1ST, AND 2ND INVERSION

D Major: root

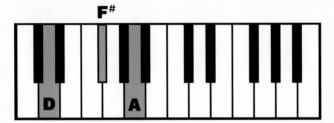 

D Major: 1st inversion

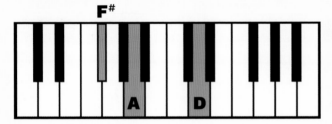 

D Major: 2nd inversion

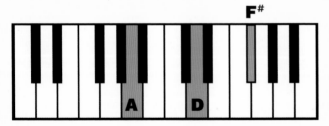 

E MAJOR, ROOT, 1ST, AND 2ND INVERSION

E Major: root

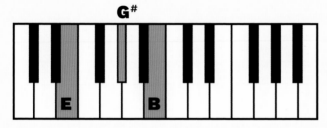
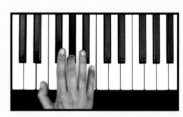

E Major: 1st inversion

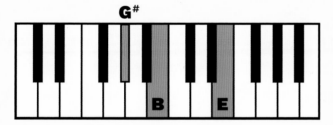

E Major: 2nd inversion

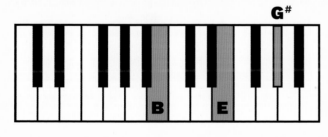

SHAPE THREE CHORDS: C# D# G#

Shape-three chords all start on the black note.

C# Major

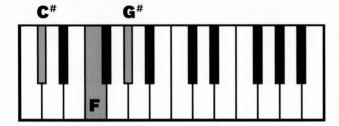 

Here is the chord of C# Major. Think of this shape as an inverted triangle, upside down, like the letter V. There is a white note in the middle, and a black note on either side.

These next two chords share the same shape.

D# Major

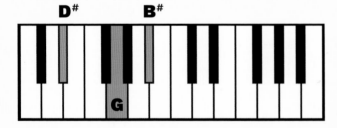 

G# Major

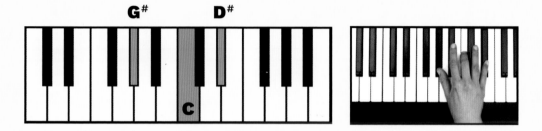

SHAPE THREE: CHORD SEQUENCE

Conduct three strikes of the chord per bar with your right hand, and one-in-the-bar with finger 1 of your left hand. On the final bar, play one nice ending chord.

	1	2	3	4		1	2	3	4		1	2	3	4		1	2	3	4
Right	C#	C#	C#		-	D#	D#	D#		-	G#	G#	G#		-	C#			
Left	C#				-	D#				-	G#				-	C#			

SHAPE THREE: INVERSIONS

Over the next few pages are your inversions for C#, D#, and G#. Now you're getting used to this, instead of striking the chord, try arpeggiating the chord—play each note individually: finger 1, then finger 3, then finger 5, up the keyboard, progressing through each of the three shapes.

C# MAJOR, ROOT, 1ST, AND 2ND INVERSION

C# Major: root

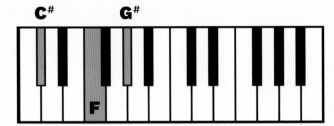 

C# Major: 1st inversion

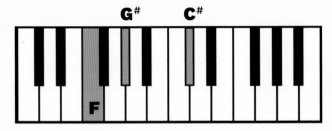 

C# Major: 2nd inversion

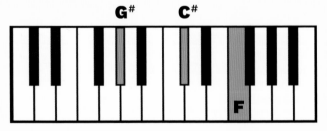 

D# MAJOR, ROOT, 1ST, AND 2ND INVERSION

D# Major: root

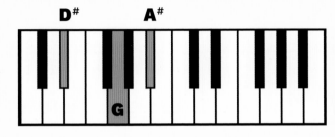

D# Major: 1st inversion

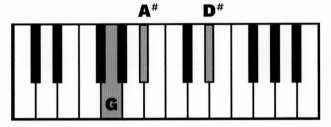

D# Major: 2nd inversion

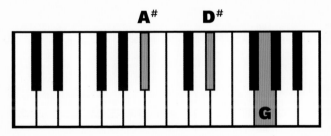

G# MAJOR, ROOT, 1ST, AND 2ND INVERSION

G# Major: root

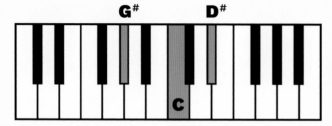 

G# Major: 1st inversion

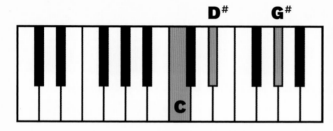 

G# Major: 2nd inversion

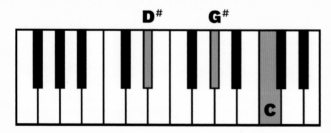 

SHAPE R CHORDS: F# A# B

On to our next shape. The Major chords you have learned so far comprise nine of the twelve Major chords that exist in the octave. We'll put them in order soon, once we have learned the final three. These final three are all a different shape to one another. I've put them together under the letter "R," which stands for "random."

F# Major

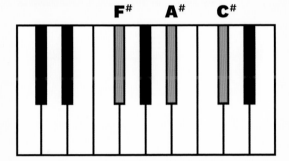 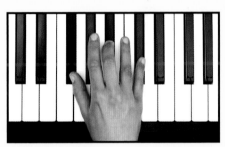

F# Major is the most easily remembered of the three, because it consists of all black notes.

A# Major

In my weekly piano sessions at Rok Skool Sussex, A# Major is the one everyone forgets. So, commit it to memory like this: black-white-white. This is the same B♭ chord from "Let it Be."

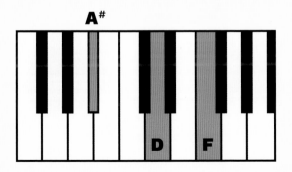 

B Major

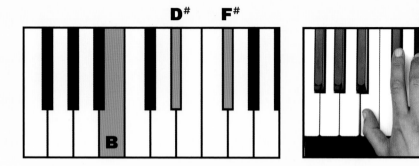

Lastly is the chord of B, which is one semitone further up the keyboard. This one is white-black-black.

SHAPE R: CHORD SEQUENCE

Play one-in-the-bar chords with the right hand, and single notes with finger 1 of your left hand, then three strikes per bar with your right. On the final bar, play one finishing chord.

	1	2	3	4		1	2	3	4		1	2	3	4		1	2	3	4
Right	F#	F#	F#		-	A#	A#	A#		-	B	B	B		-	F#			
Left	F#				-	A#				-	B				-	F#			

SHAPE R INVERSIONS

Here are the inversions for those random Major chords of F#, A#, and B. Arpeggiate the chord—play each note individually, up the keyboard, progressing through each of the three shapes.

F# MAJOR, ROOT, 1ST, AND 2ND INVERSION

F# Major: root

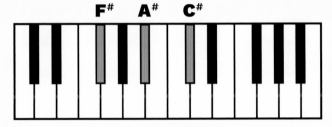

F# Major: 1st inversion

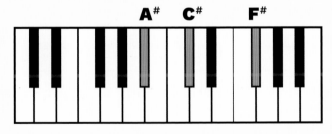

F# Major: 2nd inversion

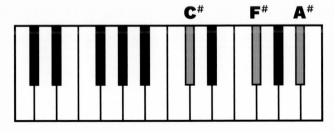

A# MAJOR, ROOT, 1ST, AND 2ND INVERSION

A# Major: root

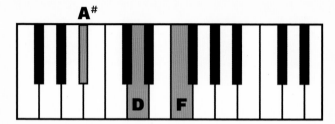 

A# Major: 1st inversion

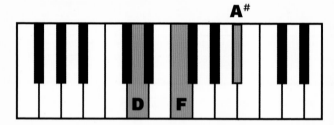 

A# Major: 2nd inversion

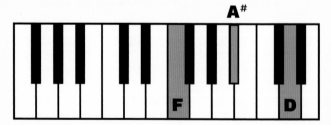 

B MAJOR, ROOT, 1ST, AND 2ND INVERSION

B Major: root

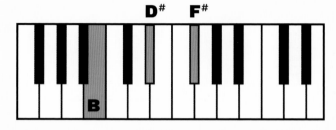 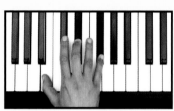

B Major: 1st inversion

B Major: 2nd inversion

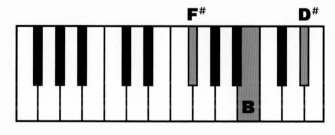 

12 MAJOR ROOT CHORDS IN ORDER

In the words of the Stylistics, let's put it all together! Your shape one, two, three, and random are now arranged in sequence, moving up the keyboard in semitones, from C to C. There are thirteen chords in this illustration, but just like with your scales (which should be seven notes instead of eight), we end with the chord you started with, one octave up, to round off your journey.

CHORDS	Notes involved	Shape
C	C, E, G	1
C#	C#, F, G#	3
D	D, F#, A	2
D#	D#, G, A#	3
E	E, G#, B	2
F	F, A, C	1
F#	F#, A#, C#	R
G	G, B, D	1
G#	G#, C, D#	3
A	A, C#, E	2
A#	A#, D, F	R
B	B, D#, F#	R

SONG SEQUENCE: COMBINING INVERSIONS

The function of inversions is to enable you to go from one chord to another with the minimum movement of your fingers. Once you get used to your Major and minor chords in all three positions—root, 1st inversion, and 2nd inversion—you will never look back. Here's a sequence to help you master the art. It is linked to a David Bowie song to which it corresponds very well, so once you are comfortable with the chord changes in each sequence, play it alongside the track. It will guide you along and keep you in time.

G – Eᵐ – A – C

There are just four chords involved in David Bowie's "Five Years," and they are played round and round for almost the whole song.

David Bowie was an inventor of characters, which he himself then inhabited. In 1972, he became Ziggy, with the release of his album *The Rise and Fall of Ziggy Stardust and The Spiders From Mars*. "Five Years" was the opening track, telling us of the immediate aftermath to an announcement that the world had just "five years left to die in."

G — E^{m 1st inv}

The inversions system gives us options. To minimize the amount of finger movement changing from one chord to the other, you are going to play G as normal, followed by E^m in the 1st inversion position, because all you have to move to change from the G to E^m in this position is one little note. Your G Major triad is GBD. Move finger 5 up one white note to change it to GBE and *voila*, you have E^m.

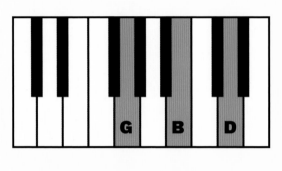
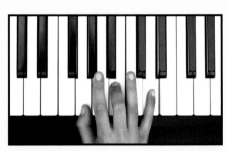

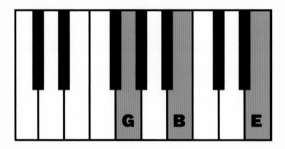

A – C 2nd inv

This is a normal A Major chord, followed by the 2nd inversion of C. Both finger 1 and finger 2 need to move downward, to change from one to the other.

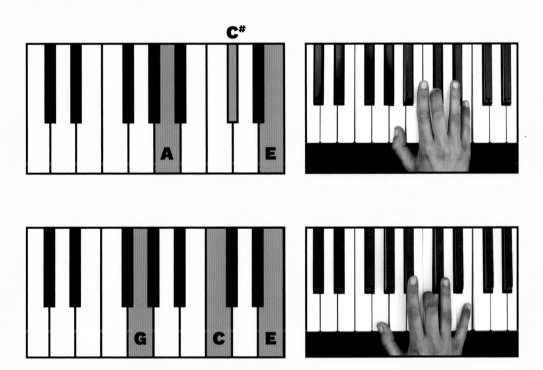

C 2nd inv G – G

Because the chord sequence is circular—after the fourth chord, you need to go back to the first—you need to move fingers 3 and 5 downward by one white note to change from the last chord, C 2nd inv, to the first chord, G.

Now try it with the track. It's a really slow "four count" with the chord on "one," so you have plenty of time from one chord to the next.

COUNTING TIME: EIGHTH BEATS

Until now, you've been counting in quarter beats—four beats to the bar: *one two three four*.

Now you need to count in this way: *one and two and three and four and*.

This is an eighth beat count, a "quaver" count. You need to know it because often, you'll be playing on one of the in between "and" beats.

Here's an eight bar, shape-one chord routine for the right hand. The E^m and E chords are both first inversions. The F, G, and A^m are all root chords. The sequence itself is simple, but the amount of times you hit the chord within the space of a bar is going to get twice as hectic, so let's work up to it.

To start, give yourself a brisk count of four and then continue at the same tempo, striking the chord on the first beat of each bar. With the left hand, play the root note of each chord as usual.

1	2	3	4		1	2	3	4		1	2	3	4		1	2	3	4
F				-	G				-	E^m				-	A^m			
1	2	3	4		1	2	3	4		1	2	3	4		1	2	3	4
F				-	G				-	E				-	A^m			

It's almost the same thing twice, except the second time around, when you get to E, it's a Major chord instead of a minor one—remember to play it in its first inversion form. Refer back to page 53 to remind yourself of the chord of E Major and its first inversion.

FOUR IN THE BAR

You're going to play the sequence again, but this time, strike the chord on each beat of the bar, so four times in every bar. In musical tempo terms, each of your chords will now be worth a quarter note or crotchet. Again, the E chords in the following table are first inversion chords.

1	2	3	4		1	2	3	4		1	2	3	4		1	2	3	4
F	F	F	F	-	G	G	G	G	-	E^m	E^m	E^m	E^m	-	A^m	A^m	A^m	A^m
1	2	3	4		1	2	3	4		1	2	3	4		1	2	3	4
F	F	F	F	-	G	G	G	G	-	E	E	E	E	-	A^m	A^m	A^m	A^m

EIGHT IN THE BAR

Play the sequence again. This time, you're doubling up the number of your right-hand strikes of the chord. Strike it on each eighth beat of the bar, so eight times in every bar.

The lengths of the bars haven't changed (you could do yourself a favor by counting them in and playing them more slowly)—but your workload within them has doubled. Once again, the E chords in the following table are first inversion chords.

	1	AND	2	AND	3	AND	4	AND		1	AND	2	AND	3	AND	4	AND
Right	F	F	F	F	F	F	F	F	-	G	G	G	G	G	G	G	G
Left	F								-	G							

	1	AND	2	AND	3	AND	4	AND		1	AND	2	AND	3	AND	4	AND
Right	E^m	E^m	E^m	E^m	E^m	E^m	E^m	E^m	-	A^m	A^m	A^m	A^m	A^m	A^m	A^m	A^m
Left	E								-	A							

	1	AND	2	AND	3	AND	4	AND		1	AND	2	AND	3	AND	4	AND
Right	F	F	F	F	F	F	F	F	-	G	G	G	G	G	G	G	G
Left	F								-	G							

	1	AND	2	AND	3	AND	4	AND		1	AND	2	AND	3	AND	4	AND
Right	E	E	E	E	E	E	E	E	-	A^m	A^m	A^m	A^m	A^m	A^m	A^m	A^m
Left	E								-	A							

Now try playing it along to the song "Bad Romance" from our divine patroness of level two.

GO GO GO—YOU'RE NOW A GAGA!

LEVEL THREE: BERLIN

Irving Berlin couldn't read a note of music—and he only played the black notes. He wrote "White Christmas," "There's No Business Like Show Business," and hundreds of other songs. Irving said by not knowing the rules, he was "free to violate them." He had a "trick" piano made for him, which had a wheel on the side to move all the strings left or right, to align a different range of notes behind the black keys. You will become just as familiar with the black notes, as level three teaches you more about sharps and flats, as well as introducing you to minor chords and six more scales.

TURNING MAJORS INTO MINORS

There is one simple rule to convert a root Major into a minor chord. Simply move the middle note of the three one semitone to the left.

Take the first chord you learned in this book, the chord of C Major, consisting of three notes from finger 1 to finger 5: C, then E, then G. To turn that C Major into C minor, the E in the middle needs to go down a semitone to E♭. Try it: play both chords and hear the dramatic difference between a Major and a minor: C – Cᵐ.

C Major

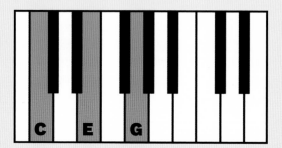 

C minor

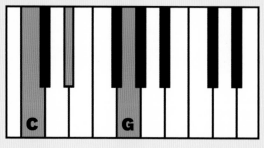 

Try playing it where you move instantly from the first chord to the second. Sound familiar? It should remind you of "Thus Spake Zarathustra," the theme from *2001: A Space Odyssey*, the music Elvis used to come out to before his performances.

Try it with another chord you learned at the beginning: F Major. It consists of three notes from bottom to top: F, A, and C.

What is the middle note? A. Apply the rule now. "Flatten" it by a semitone, which is done by going to the black note immediately before it, an A flat. Play the F Major chord, followed by the F minor.

F Major

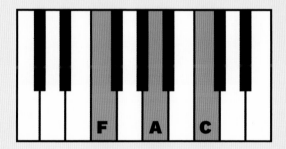 

F minor

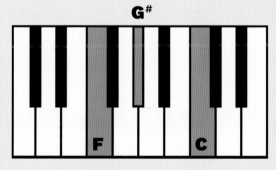 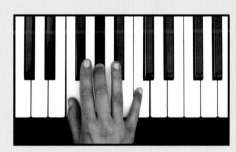

Do it fast: F Major, F minor. I'm sorry, but much as he'd like to come out to your fanfare, Elvis has left the building.

You can apply that rule—of shifting the middle note down a semitone—to every single one of the twelve Major root chords that you know, thus turning them into minors, and at a single stroke, turning twelve chords into twenty-four.

You have already come across three of these minors in shape-one chords: A minor, D minor, and E minor. Here are the other nine, arranged into similar groups.

SHAPE FOUR MINOR CHORDS: Cᵐ, Fᵐ, Gᵐ

These three minor chords share the same shape—remember them as shape four.

C minor

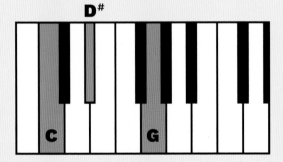

F minor

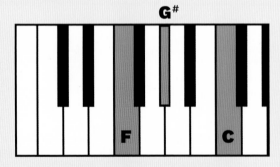

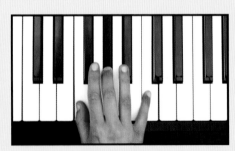

G minor

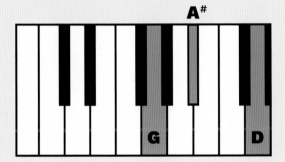 

Play them in sequence:

	1	2	3	4		1	2	3	4
Right	C^m	C^m	C^m		-	F^m	F^m	F^m	
Left	C				-	F			

	1	2	3	4		1	2	3	4
Right	G^m	G^m	G^m	G^m	-	C^m			
Left	G				-	C			

Then play them in inversions—you know how to do it by now.

SHAPE FIVE MINOR CHORDS: C#m, F#m, G#m

These three minor chords also share the same shape—they are shape five.

C# minor

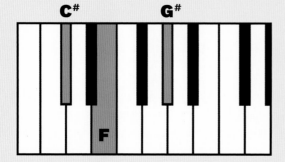

F# minor

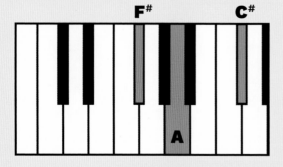

G♯ minor

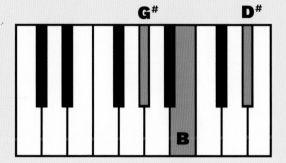

Play them in sequence, and then play them in inversions:

	1	2	3	4		1	2	3	4
Right	C♯m	C♯m	C♯m		-	F♯m	F♯m	F♯m	
Left	C♯				-	F♯			

	1	2	3	4		1	2	3	4
Right	G♯m	G♯m	G♯m		-	C♯m			
Left	G♯				-	C♯			

RANDOM MINORS: D#m, A#m, Bm

Which leaves three loners . . .

· ·

D# minor

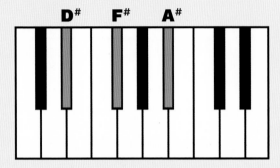

· ·

A# minor

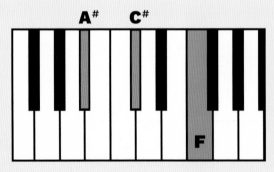

B minor

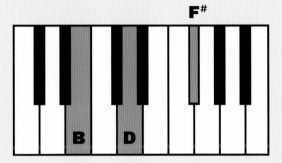

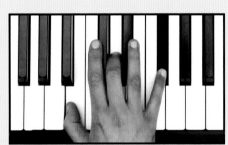

Play them in sequence, and then in inversions:

	1	2	3	4		1	2	3	4
Right	D#m	D#m	D#m		-	A#m	A#m	A#m	
Left	D#				-	A#			

	1	2	3	4		1	2	3	4
Right	Bm	Bm	Bm		-	D#m			
Left	B				-	D#			

12 MINOR ROOT CHORDS IN ORDER

Armed with those minor chords and in the words of that same Stylistics song from the 1970s, let's put it all together!

CHORDS	Notes involved	Shape
C^m	C, D$^\sharp$, G	4
C$^{\sharp m}$	C$^\sharp$, E, G$^\sharp$	5
D^m	D, F, A	1
D$^{\sharp m}$	D$^\sharp$, F$^\sharp$, A$^\sharp$	R
E^m	E, G, B	1
F^m	F, G$^\sharp$, C	4
F$^{\sharp m}$	F$^\sharp$, A, C$^\sharp$	5
G^m	G, A$^\sharp$, D	4
G$^{\sharp m}$	G$^\sharp$, B, D$^\sharp$	5
A^m	A, C, E	1
A$^{\sharp m}$	A$^\sharp$, C$^\sharp$, F	R
B^m	B, D, F$^\sharp$	R

The most important chords in a song are the first and last one (which are usually the same chord). Many a musical artist has written or performed a song starting on a moody minor. There are thousands, but I can think of no better example than the great Nina Simone and her cover of "I Put a Spell on You."

"I Put a Spell on You" was written by Screamin' Jay Hawkins in the late 1950s and made famous by Nina Simone in 1965. Nina was a virtuoso classical pianist and when first employed to play piano in a bar, she was told to sing if she wanted to keep her job. She had never sung before, but she needed the job, so she improvised vocals over the pieces she was playing and a star was born.

MAJOR/MINOR CHORD MIX ONE: D^m – G^m – $A^\#$ – A

You are playing this traveling in an upward direction until the last chord, when you come down a semitone. This chord sequence could actually be a song, but I'm not going to tell you what it is until you can play it! Get these chords together quickly, with the help of your stickers. You could assign a different sticker color to each of the four chords involved and use stickers for the left-hand notes, for instance. For the right hand, you could use stickers for the finger 1 note for each of these root chords. It might also help to write the name of the note upon the stickers.

D minor

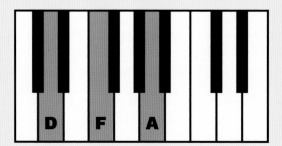
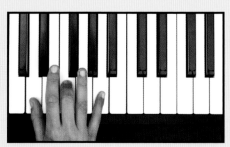

G minor

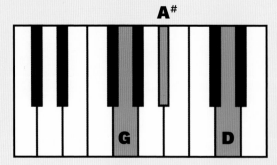

A# Major

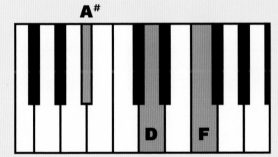

A Major

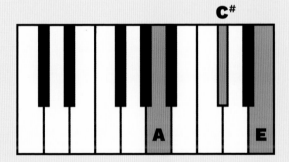

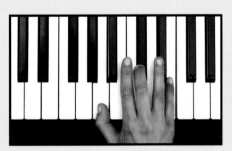

You are being pushed to slightly higher heights with each new sequence in this book. Here, for instance, not only are you mixing Majors with minors more frequently, but you have also lost that last-beat-of-the-bar vacation you've had, where you had the whole of that last beat to find the next chord, with the luxury of not having to play at the same time. This time, you're striking the chord on all four beats of the bar and moving straight to the next chord for the first beat of the next bar.

Once again, finger 1 on your left hand will be playing the root note of the chord on the first beat and holding the note down for the whole bar (so, only striking once), while your right hand is busy striking down on every beat (so, four times). Take note: each chord lasts for two bars before it changes, not one.

	1	2	3	4		1	2	3	4		1	2	3	4		1	2	3	4
Right	Dᵐ	Dᵐ	Dᵐ	Dᵐ	-	Dᵐ	Dᵐ	Dᵐ	Dᵐ	-	Gᵐ	Gᵐ	Gᵐ	Gᵐ	-	Gᵐ	Gᵐ	Gᵐ	Gᵐ
Left	D				-	D				-	G				-	G			

	1	2	3	4		1	2	3	4		1	2	3	4		1	2	3	4
Right	A#	A#	A#	A#	-	A#	A#	A#	A#	-	A	A	A	A	-	A	A	A	A
Left	A#				-	A#				-	A				-	A			

That sequence you've just played matches up beautifully with the piano part on the Amy Winehouse classic "Back to Black." Try playing along with it—you're getting to the point now where that simplest and greatest of pleasures is on your musical horizon, playing along with a number you know and love. And if you can sing and don't mind unveiling your emerging skills to friends and family, well—you have a live number!

Amy Winehouse had a tattoo that read "Blake's" above a pocket design on her chest. When she and Blake broke up, Amy wrote this song with producer Mark Ronson. "He went back to his girlfriend," Amy said of Blake, "and I went back to black—the dark times, the booze." The misery may have helped sweeten the next year for her, though—in 2007, *Back to Black* became one of the biggest-selling albums worldwide.

MAJOR/MINOR CHORD MIX TWO: D#m – G#m – A#

This sequence sounds like a song that will be revealed shortly and is almost identical to the last one, except it involves more black note action. But there are only three different chords this time—it's a four-chord sequence that starts and ends on the same chord.

Again, you could mark up the first notes of each chord for your right hand with the stickers. Likewise, mark each of your left-hand root notes that you need to land on (up to now, I've assigned your left-hand notes to finger 1, but it honestly doesn't matter which finger you play them with, for now). Use different-colored stickers for each chord, and if it helps, write the names of the notes upon them.

D# minor

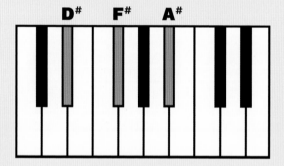
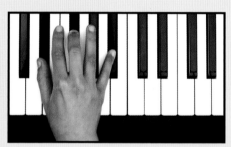

G# minor

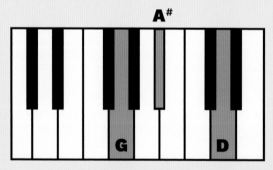

A# Major

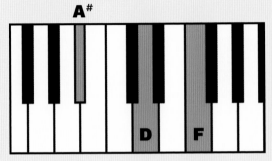

Got it? Here we go, four strikes per bar with the right hand, one strike per bar with the left, each chord lasting for two bars.

	1	2	3	4		1	2	3	4		1	2	3	4		1	2	3	4
Right	D#m	D#m	D#m	D#m	-	D#m	D#m	D#m	D#m	-	G#m	G#m	G#m	G#m		G#m	G#m	G#m	G#m
Left	D#				-	D#				-	G#				-	G#			

	1	2	3	4		1	2	3	4		1	2	3	4		1	2	3	4
Right	A#	A#	A#	A#	-	A#	A#	A#	A#	-	D#m	D#m	D#m	D#m		D#m	D#m	D#m	D#m
Left	A#				-	A#				-	D#				-	D#			

The chord sequence you've just learned sounds a lot like Pixie Lott's pop hit "Mama Do." Play along with it—it's a great fit. It's faster. It will up your speed—or tempo, as you need to call it—now you are becoming a musician!

Like the guy putting plates up on sticks at the circus, your chord plate is now spinning and singing like a flying saucer. Time to turn your attention back to the musical scales plate, which is wobbling dangerously.

You know the scale of C Major—eight nice and tidy white notes in a row. You know how to determine the three **primary chords** associated with that key and the three **relative minors** associated with the chords. You also know how to play them in their inversion positions—yes? I'm confident you're well in charge of the C Major scale, so let's continue.

Coming up over the next few pages are two more Major scales, each involving just one black note, because I'm easing you in gently. As you move through the levels, more will be introduced.

"Mama Do" was Pixie Lott's debut single. "I was in bed at Mom and Dad's, on my laptop," she said, "and I got a phone call from my A&R man. He really dragged it out." He told her she was number one. "I ran around the house screaming!" She was 18, and the first female British artist to debut straight in at number one who hadn't arrived via a television talent show.

SCALE OF G MAJOR: ONE SHARP

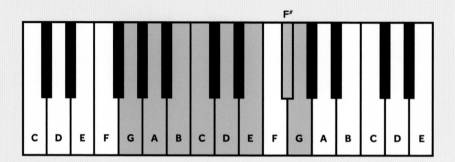

The black note involved in this eight-note scale of G Major is the seventh. Remember the correct fingering for playing a scale: your right hand plays the first three notes with your first three fingers, then you move finger 1 to the fourth note of the scale and use your whole hand to play the remaining five notes, from finger 1 to finger 5, as these images illustrate.

G Major: first 3 notes (right hand)

G Major: last 5 notes (right hand)

Play it in reverse now, from the top note back down to the bottom note. All five fingers, then finger 3 to finger 1 for the last three notes.

However, when playing a scale with the left hand, you must do the opposite. Play the first five notes with all five fingers (from finger 5 through to finger 1) followed by the last three notes with fingers 3, 2, then 1. This is illustrated in the two images below. When you've mastered it, here's a final challenge: play the scale simultaneously with both hands. It's a bit like rubbing your tummy and patting your head at the same time, but you'll get used to it after a few run-throughs.

G Major: first 5 notes (left hand)

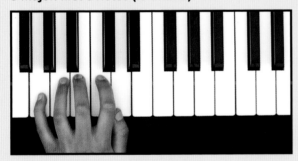

G Major: last 3 notes (left hand)

It's tricky playing both at once, so try it slowly at first, then speed it up.

SCALE OF G MAJOR—THREE PRIMARY MAJORS:
G, C, D

Remember the rule: make a Major chord on the first, the fourth, and the fifth. Identify the first: G, the fourth: C, and the fifth: D.

Turn them into Major chords. The first two are shape one, the last one is shape two.

Now play them, two beats on each bar. Count yourself in, aloud and slowly, to give yourself time, and keep counting, as you go through the routine. Play the root note of each chord with the left hand.

1	2	3	4		1	2	3	4		1
G		C		-	D		C		-	G

SCALE OF G MAJOR—THREE RELATIVE MINORS:
E^m, A^m, B^m

Again, the rule—from the Major chord, go down three semitones from the root note (the one under finger 1) and whatever note you land on, turn it into a minor chord.

Our first chord—the root—was G. From there, go down one semitone. That note is G flat. Then F, then E. You're there, on E, three semitones descended from the G. Now make a minor chord there: E minor.

The fourth was a C—down three semitones and you land on A. So your chord is A^m. The fifth was a D—down three semitones and you land on B. So your chord is B^m.

Factoring those three relative minors in, here we are with our six great chords in the key of G, the positive Majors, the melancholy minors, all hand in glove with one another, giving you the perfect framework with which to write songs or improvise in that key— that's something to look forward to. For now, just play them, like this:

1	2	3	4		1	2	3	4		1	2	3	4		1
G		E^m		-	C		A^m		-	D		B^m		-	G

SCALE OF F MAJOR: ONE FLAT

This black note lives in the F Major scale under its flat name. The big question as to why it's a flat and not a sharp will be answered soon. But for now, just accept this and move on.

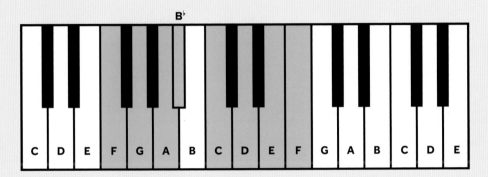

The black note involved in this eight-note scale of F Major is the fourth. The right hand uses different fingers, finger 1 to finger 4.

Play it up and down, then try it with both hands. If you want to be a decent pianist, this is you in keyboard gym, toughening up. Remember, unlike your right hand, your left hand plays the first five notes from finger 5 to finger 1, then the last three. Like this:

F Major: first 5 notes (left hand)

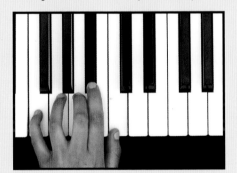

F Major: last 3 notes (left hand)

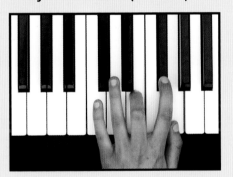

SCALE OF F MAJOR—THREE PRIMARY MAJORS:

F, B$^\flat$, C

Make a Major chord on the first, the fourth, and the fifth.

1	2	3	4		1	2	3	4		1
F		B$^\flat$		-	C		B$^\flat$		-	F

SCALE OF F MAJOR—THREE RELATIVE MINORS:

D^m, G^m, A^m

Go down three semitones from the root note of the Major chord and whichever note you land on, turn it into a minor chord. By now, you're probably tuning in to the fact that some of these Major chords are reappearing in different keys and different scenarios, and are bringing their relative minors along with them. C Major's relative minor will always be A minor. Likewise, all the others you are becoming used to will follow suit. So, here's the sequence of six chords: three Major, three minor, belonging to the key of F Major.

1	2	3	4		1	2	3	4		1	2	3	4		1
F		D^m		-	B$^\flat$		G^m		-	C		A^m		-	F

SHARPS AND FLATS

So, to the big question: when do we call it a sharp and when do we call it a flat? It's all about two things that are unchangeable in music:

1. The alphabetical order of the letters: **A – B – C – D – E – F – G**

2. The intervals of semitones between the notes of the scale: **2 2 1 2 2 2 1**

WHEN IS IT A FLAT?

Look at the scale you have just been familiarizing yourself with—**F Major**. Alphabetically, we start from the F, so the alphabetical order of the notes has to be:

F – G – A – B – C – D – E – F

Now apply the "intervals."

* Between the F and G: two semitones—this is our first **2**.

* Between G and A: two semitones—this is our second **2** checked off the list.

* Between A and B: two semitones? No! It should only be **1**. So, we need to bring it *down* by a semitone. And when we bring a note down a semitone, we *flatten* it. So the B becomes B flat, and our intervals formula is obeyed.

* Between B♭ and C: **2** semitones. Check.

* Between C and D: **2** semitones. Check.

* Between D and E: **2** semitones. Check.

* Between E and F: **1** semitone. Check.

WHEN IS IT A SHARP?

Look at the only scale you have learned so far with a sharp in it, the scale of **G Major**. Alphabetically, we start from the G, so the alphabetical order of the notes has to be:

G – A – B – C – D – E – F – G

Now let's apply the "intervals."

* Between G and A: **2** semitones. Check.

* Between A and B: **2** semitones. Check.

* Between B and C: **1** semitone. Check.

* Between C and D: **2** semitones. Check.

* Between D and E: **2** semitones. Check.

* Between E and F: only one semitone, when it should be two! So, we need to take it up by a semitone. And when we take a note up a semitone, we sharpen it. So, the F becomes F sharp, and our intervals formula is obeyed. Now the interval is **2**.

* Finally, between F# and G: **1** semitone. Check.

FOUR MORE SCALES: D, A, E, B

Let's look at four more scales, the first with two sharps involved, the next with three, then four, then five. In each case, practice the scale two-handed up and down. Fill in the missing chords in the familiar sequence of the Major located on the first and its relative minor, then the Major on the fourth and its relative minor, then the Major on the fifth and its relative minor. Play it, too, with the root note using the left hand.

....

Scale of D Major: two sharps

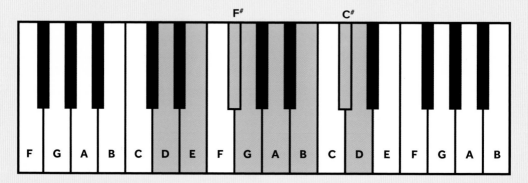

Test yourself: D Major

1. What are the three primary Majors?
2. What are their three relative minors?
3. In which position of the scale are the sharps located?
4. Why are they sharps and not flats?
5. Can you provide the missing chords in the sequence?

1	2	3	4		1	2	3	4		1	2	3	4		1
D		?		-	?		?		-	?		?		-	D

Answers: 1. D, G, A; **2.** Bm, Em, F♯m; **3.** 3 and 7; **4.** To obey the intervals rule, they need "sharpening," not "flattening." **5.** Bm, G, Em, A, F♯m

Scale of A Major: three sharps

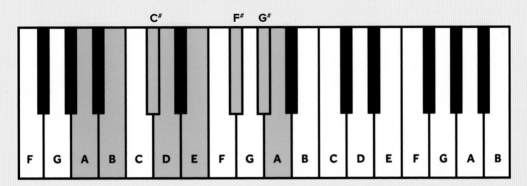

C#   F# G#

F | G | A | B | C | D | E | F | G | A | B | C | D | E | F | G | A | B

Test yourself: A Major

1. What are the three primary Majors?
2. What are their three relative minors?
3. In which position of the scale are the sharps located?
4. Why are they sharps and not flats?
5. Can you provide the missing chords in the sequence?

1	2	3	4		1	2	3	4		1	2	3	4		1
A		?		-	?		?		-	?		?		-	A

Answers: 1. A, D, E; 2. F#m, Bm, C#m; 3. 3, 6, and 7; 4. To obey the intervals rule, they need "sharpening," not "flattening;" 5. F#m, D, Bm, E C#m

Scale of E Major: four sharps

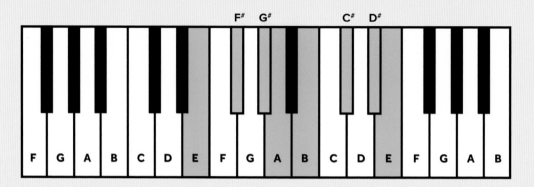

Test yourself: E Major

1. What are the three primary Majors?
2. What are their three relative minors?
3. In which position of the scale are the sharps located?
4. Can you provide the missing chords in the sequence?

1	2	3	4		1	2	3	4		1	2	3	4		1
E		?		-	?		?		-	?		?		-	E

Answers: 1. E, A, B; **2.** C#m, F#m, G#m; **3.** 2, 3, 6, and 7; **4.** C#m, A, F#m, B, G#m

98

Scale of B Major: five sharps

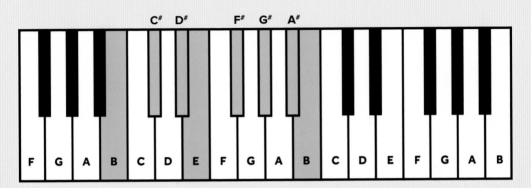

C# D#   F# G# A#

F | G | A | B | C | D | E | F | G | A | B | C | D | E | F | G | A | B

Test yourself: B Major

1. What are the three primary Majors?
2. What are their three relative minors?
3. In which position of the scale are the sharps located?
4. Can you provide the missing chords in the sequence?

1	2	3	4		1	2	3	4		1	2	3	4			1
B		?		-	?		?		-	?		?		-		B

When you practice the B Major scale, try using finger 4 to finger 1 with the left hand, as this is more comfortable.

MOVING YOUR LEFT HAND

Here's an exercise where your left hand is four times as busy as your right. While your right hand holds down the chord for all four beats of the bar, your left hand plays a single note on each of those four beats.

Start with the chords in your right hand, played against a slow count of four. Move upward to the F, further upward to the G, and down for the C. It's two bars on each chord, until the bit at the end. Slow count of four first, then continue at the same tempo:

Right hand:

1	2	3	4		1	2	3	4		1	2	3	4		1	2	3	4	
C				-	C				-	F				-	F				-

1	2	3	4		1	2	3	4		1	2	3	4		1	2	3	4	
G				-	G				-	C		F		-	G				-

The left-hand part is basically a descending scale of C. Remember, these are single notes, not chords. You are pressing the note on each beat of the bar. Each note is played twice, then you move down one white note to play the next note (twice):

Left hand:

1	2	3	4		1	2	3	4		1	2	3	4		1	2	3	4	
C	C	B	B	-	A	A	G	G	-	F	F	E	E	-	D	D	C	C	-

1	2	3	4		1	2	3	4		1	2	3	4		1	2	3	4	
G	G	F	F	-	E	E	D	D	-	C	E	F	F	-	G	G	A	B	-

It gets a little bit more hectic in the last two bars. Try them together. Position your right hand on a C chord, and your left-hand finger 1 on a C note. During the exercise, your hands will be traveling in opposite directions.

	1	2	3	4		1	2	3	4		1	2	3	4		1	2	3	4
Right	C					C					F					F			
Left	C	C	B	B	-	A	A	G	G	-	F	F	E	E	-	D	D	C	C

	1	2	3	4		1	2	3	4		1	2	3	4		1	2	3	4
Right	G					G					C		F			G			
Left	G	G	F	F	-	E	E	D	D	-	C	E	F	F	-	G	G	A	B

There was a great old Procol Harum song that used a similar progression: "A Whiter Shade of Pale." Play along with it, and you'll find this two-handed piano sequence will soon come together. Another song with more or less the same sequence is Percy Sledge's soul classic, "When a Man Loves a Woman."

WELCOME TO LEVEL FOUR—YOU'RE A BERLIN!

"A Whiter Shade of Pale" was the United Kingdom's number one song in 1967. Procol Harum's Gary Brooker, the composer, based it on a piece of classical music: Bach's "Air on a G String." Meanwhile, the organist on the track, Matthew Fisher, after a long legal battle, successfully sued for a share of the royalties 40 years later.

LEVEL FOUR: JOOLS

Of Jools Holland, bluesman B. B. King said: "I didn't think anyone could play like that. That left hand never stops." For that matter, neither does the right hand, and when they come together . . . wow! "You have your ten fingers," Jools says, "which become the ten members of the orchestra." He learned to play by ear before he ever learned any theory, and he is the ideal artist for our penultimate level. Here, we widen your chord base dramatically by slightly adapting the chords you already know to introduce you to a range of new chord families.

CHORD FAMILIES

So far, your chords have been grouped into shapes. Now it's time to arrange them into their proper family groups. Just as families look alike, so chord families sound alike. Just as families obey the same rules . . . okay, there my family analogy breaks down!

A triad is the name we give to the three notes of our chord. All of the chords you've encountered so far have been made up of the first, third, and fifth note of the scale to which they belong. The chords you encounter now, though still three-note combinations, will involve other notes of the scale.

We have been here before, when we flattened the middle note of your first chords, to turn them into a minor. It changed the tone and color . . . and how!

We are going to move those first, third, and fifth notes around some more, in half steps or whole steps—meaning, we are going to move one of those three notes either a semitone or a tone, thereby creating a whole new-sounding chord. You already have minors and Majors at your fingertips. Through changing one note (as you did from Major to minor), you will find yourself playing suspended seconds and fourths, Major 7ths and dominant 7ths, diminished and augmented chords, each family group with a sound and vibe of its own. These types of chord don't belong to the classical era—they are the foundation stones of the rock, pop, and jazz age to which we belong.

Here they are, from A to G (seven versions), in their various family forms. In each case, remind yourself of the scale before you play the chord, so you get the sense of it. Follow the illustrations and images laid out here and use your stickers, as and when you need to.

SUS 4S

This is standard musician-speak in the pop/rock world. Sus 4s is short for suspended fourths. As I say, your chords thus far have comprised the first, third, and fifth of the scale, but in each of these family groups, one of those three is about to change. This family group replaces the third with the fourth.

A ^{sus4}

A **sus4**

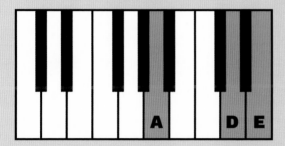
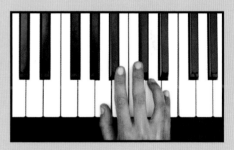

Typically in pop, it is used in conjunction with a normal A Major chord, like this:

1	2	3	4		1	2	3	4
A sus4	A sus4	A sus4	A	-				

1	2	3	4		1	2	3	4
A sus4	A sus4	A sus4	A	-				

Count it in at a lively pace, then keep counting as you play a full bar, count an empty bar, play a full bar, count an empty bar. You'll note that only finger 4 needs to move. It's on the D (fourth note of the A scale) for the sus 4 chord, then down a semitone for the A chord. Also notice that the A chord is the "resolve"—i.e., it provides a kind of resolution to the suspended chord before it.

B ^{sus4}

You learned the B scale with its five sharps at the end of the previous level. Go through it now, until you come to the fourth note (an E). That note provides the suspended fourth in this chord.

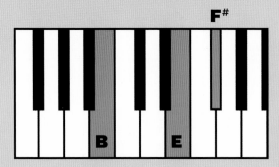

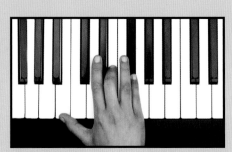

The suspended fourth note then resolves to the third note of the scale for the B Major. Again, count yourself in at a lively pace, then keep counting aloud through the first bar when you're playing, the second when you're not, the third when you're playing, the fourth when you're not:

1	2	3	4		1	2	3	4
B ^{sus4}	B ^{sus4}	B ^{sus4}	B	-				

1	2	3	4		1	2	3	4
B ^{sus4}	B ^{sus4}	B ^{sus4}	B	-				

Now put the A and B together in sequence. Try this:

1	2	3	4		1	2	3	4
A ^{sus4}	A ^{sus4}	A ^{sus4}	A	-				

1	2	3	4		1	2	3	4
B ^{sus4}	B ^{sus4}	B ^{sus4}	B	-				

THE FINAL FIVE: C sus4, D sus4, E sus4, F sus4, G sus4

Here are the final five. Just play the "sus 4 and resolve" sequence once, now that you're getting used to it:

....

C sus4

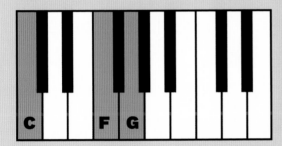 

1	2	3	4		1	2	3	4
C sus4	C sus4	C sus4	C	-				

....

D sus4

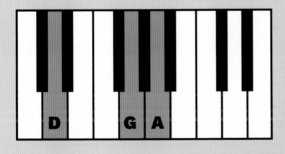 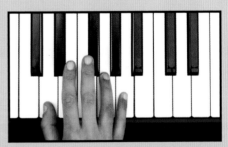

1	2	3	4		1	2	3	4
D sus4	D sus4	D sus4	D	-				

E ^{sus4}

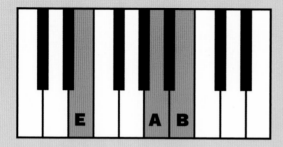

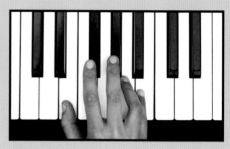

1	2	3	4		1	2	3	4
E ^{sus4}	E ^{sus4}	E ^{sus4}	E	-				

F ^{sus4}

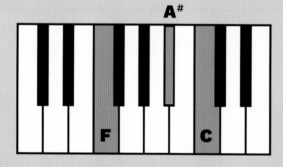

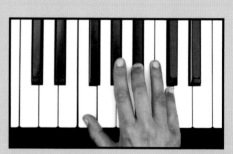

1	2	3	4		1	2	3	4
F ^{sus4}	F ^{sus4}	F ^{sus4}	F	-				

G sus4

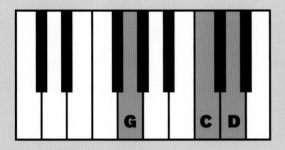

1	2	3	4		1	2	3	4
G sus4	G sus4	G sus4	G	-				

SUS 4 CHORD SEQUENCE

Next is a sus 4 sequence that works very well when played along with a familiar song. Your right hand plays F Major and F sus4 and . . . that's it, literally, all the way through the song! The notes you play with the left hand are what change the sound of the two repetitive chords on the right and turn them into something else.

You alternate between the Major and the sus 4 with your right hand very quickly, and strike the chord eight times in each bar. So, count yourself in at a lively pace, *one* **and** *two* **and** *three* **and** *four* **and**. Then practice striking the F Major chord on each word as you count. Where the **and** is highlighted—that's where you play the sus 4. With the left hand, simply play the note of F on the first beat of the bar.

	1	AND	2	AND	3	AND	4	AND		1	AND	2	AND	3	AND	4	AND
Right	F	F	F	F sus4	F	F	F	F sus4	-	F	F	F	F sus4	F	F	F	F sus4
Left	F								-	F							

That's the first two bars. On the next two bars, simply change the note you play with the left hand to a D.

	1	AND	2	AND	3	AND	4	AND		1	AND	2	AND	3	AND	4	AND
Right	F	F	F	F sus4	F	F	F	F sus4	-	F	F	F	F sus4	F	F	F	F sus4
Left	D								-	D							

Keep your left hand heading down the keyboard as you find your next note, a B♭, for bars five and six of this eight-bar sequence.

	1	AND	2	AND	3	AND	4	AND		1	AND	2	AND	3	AND	4	AND
Right	F	F	F	F sus4	F	F	F	F sus4	-	F	F	F	F sus4	F	F	F	F sus4
Left	B♭								-	B♭							

For the last two bars, simply go back to F with the left hand and repeat the first two bars.

Although this sus 4 sequence is not exactly what is played on the record, it works well when played along with the Bruno Mars track "Just the Way You Are."

The 2010 Bruno Mars single "Just the Way You Are" hit number one in the United States. He wasn't trying to be deep, he said, he was a fan of simple songs, especially the thousands of doo-wop songs where "it's the same four chords." Bruno declares himself a big fan of 1950s Elvis, who would "go on stage and scare people because he was such a force!"

MORE SUS 4 CHORD SEQUENCES

In the following sequences, the chords are arranged into the primary Major groupings associated with a particular scale.

Give yourself the usual fast four-beat count in and keep counting as you play.

SUS 4 SEQUENCE IN THE KEY OF A: A–D–E–A

1	2	3	4		1	2	3	4
A sus4	A sus4	A sus4	A	-				

1	2	3	4		1	2	3	4
D sus4	D sus4	D sus4	D	-				

1	2	3	4		1	2	3	4
E sus4	E sus4	E sus4	E	-				

1	2	3	4		1	2	3	4
A sus4	A sus4	A sus4	A	-				

SUS 4 SEQUENCE IN THE KEY OF C: C–F–G–C

1	2	3	4		1	2	3	4
C sus4	C sus4	C sus4	C	-				

1	2	3	4		1	2	3	4
F sus4	F sus4	F sus4	F	-				

1	2	3	4		1	2	3	4
G sus4	G sus4	G sus4	G	-				

1	2	3	4		1	2	3	4
C sus4	C sus4	C sus4	C	-				

SUS 4 SEQUENCE IN THE KEY OF D: D–G–A–D

1	2	3	4		1	2	3	4
D sus4	D sus4	D sus4	D	-				

1	2	3	4		1	2	3	4
G sus4	G sus4	G sus4	G	-				

1	2	3	4		1	2	3	4
A sus4	A sus4	A sus4	A	-				

1	2	3	4		1	2	3	4
D sus4	D sus4	D sus4	D	-				

SUS 4 SEQUENCE IN THE KEY OF E: E–A–B–E

1	2	3	4		1	2	3	4
E sus4	E sus4	E sus4	E	-				

1	2	3	4		1	2	3	4
A sus4	A sus4	A sus4	A	-				

1	2	3	4		1	2	3	4
B sus4	B sus4	B sus4	B	-				

1	2	3	4		1	2	3	4
E sus4	E sus4	E sus4	E	-				

SUS 2S

This is muso-speak for suspended seconds. Sus 2 chords are the root, the second, and the fifth. Familiarize yourself with this family group:

A ^{sus2}

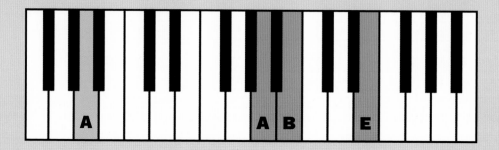

1	2	3	4		1	2	3	4
A sus2	A sus2	A sus2	A	-				

B ^{sus2}

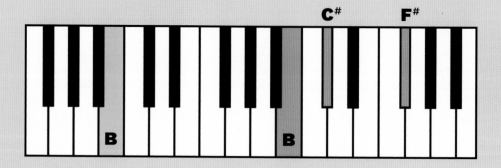

1	2	3	4		1	2	3	4
B sus2	B sus2	B sus2	B	-				

C ^{sus2}

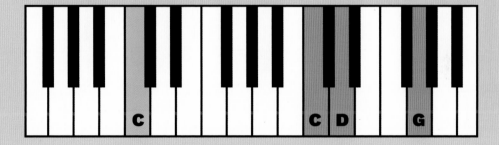

1	2	3	4		1	2	3	4
C sus2	C sus2	C sus2	C	-				

D ^{sus2}

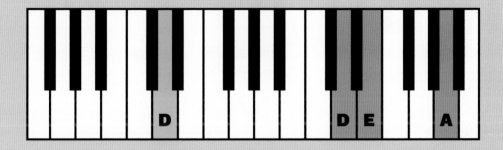

1	2	3	4		1	2	3	4
D sus2	D sus2	D sus2	D	-				

E ^{sus2}

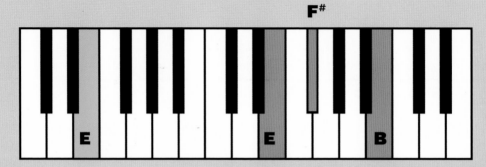

1	2	3	4		1	2	3	4
E sus2	E sus2	E sus2	E	-				

F ^{sus2}

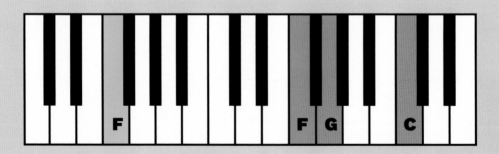

1	2	3	4		1	2	3	4
F sus2	F sus2	F sus2	F	-				

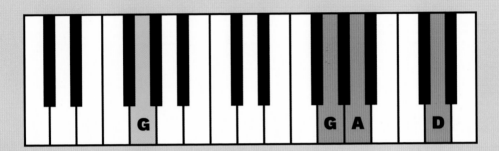

1	2	3	4		1	2	3	4
G sus2	G sus2	G sus2	G	-				

SUS 2 AND SUS 4 CHORD SEQUENCES

In the following sequences, the chords are once again arranged into primary Major groupings associated with a particular scale. This time, we play each chord as a sus 2 first, then as a sus 4, each time resolving to the Major. Play it quickly! A fast four-beat count in and keep counting as you play. Pay close attention to the small 2s and 4s in the diagram.

In these next four sequences, over the following pages, you will be playing chord groupings in four different keys.

CHORD SEQUENCE ONE

Sus 2 and sus 4 sequence, A scale: A – D – E – A

1	2	3	4		1	2	3	4
A sus2	A sus2	A sus2	A	-				

1	2	3	4		1	2	3	4
A sus4	A sus4	A sus4	A	-				

1	2	3	4		1	2	3	4
D sus2	D sus2	D sus2	D	-				

1	2	3	4		1	2	3	4
D sus4	D sus4	D sus4	D	-				

1	2	3	4		1	2	3	4
E sus2	E sus2	E sus2	E	-				

1	2	3	4		1	2	3	4
E sus4	E sus4	E sus4	E	-				

1	2	3	4		1	2	3	4
A sus2	A sus2	A sus2	A	-				

1	2	3	4		1	2	3	4
A sus4	A sus4	A sus4	A	-				

CHORD SEQUENCE TWO

Sus 2 and sus 4 sequence, C scale: C – F – G – C

1	2	3	4		1	2	3	4
C sus2	C sus2	C sus2	C	-				

1	2	3	4		1	2	3	4
C sus4	C sus4	C sus4	C	-				

1	2	3	4		1	2	3	4
F sus2	F sus2	F sus2	F	-				

1	2	3	4		1	2	3	4
F sus4	F sus4	F sus4	F	-				

1	2	3	4		1	2	3	4
G sus2	G sus2	G sus2	G	-				

1	2	3	4		1	2	3	4
G sus4	G sus4	G sus4	G	-				

1	2	3	4		1	2	3	4
C sus2	C sus2	C sus2	C	-				

1	2	3	4		1	2	3	4
C sus4	C sus4	C sus4	C	-				

CHORD SEQUENCE THREE

Sus 2 and sus 4 sequence, D scale: D – G – A – D

1	2	3	4		1	2	3	4
D sus2	D sus2	D sus2	D	-				

1	2	3	4		1	2	3	4
D sus4	D sus4	D sus4	D	-				

1	2	3	4		1	2	3	4
G sus2	G sus2	G sus2	G	-				

1	2	3	4		1	2	3	4
G sus4	G sus4	G sus4	G	-				

1	2	3	4		1	2	3	4
A sus2	A sus2	A sus2	A	-				

1	2	3	4		1	2	3	4
A sus4	A sus4	A sus4	A	-				

1	2	3	4		1	2	3	4
D sus2	D sus2	D sus2	D	-				

1	2	3	4		1	2	3	4
D sus4	D sus4	D sus4	D	-				

CHORD SEQUENCE FOUR

Sus 2 and sus 4 sequence, E scale: E – A – B – E

1	2	3	4		1	2	3	4
E sus2	E sus2	E sus2	E	-				

1	2	3	4		1	2	3	4
E sus4	E sus4	E sus4	E	-				

1	2	3	4		1	2	3	4
A sus2	A sus2	A sus2	A	-				

1	2	3	4		1	2	3	4
A sus4	A sus4	A sus4	A	-				

1	2	3	4		1	2	3	4
B sus2	B sus2	B sus2	B	-				

1	2	3	4		1	2	3	4
B sus4	B sus4	B sus4	B	-				

1	2	3	4		1	2	3	4
E sus2	E sus2	E sus2	E	-				

1	2	3	4		1	2	3	4
E sus4	E sus4	E sus4	E	-				

MAJOR 6THS

Here is another chord family. To play a Major 6th is very simple. Go back to your Major root chord, which comprised the first, third, and fifth note of the scale. To turn that chord into a Major 6th, just move the fifth up one whole step. That means a full tone, not a semitone or half step.

Here's your chord of C Major:

C Major

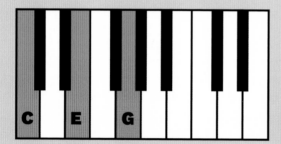

Take that fifth note (if you need to remind yourself which of the three is the fifth, simply play the first five notes of the C Major scale) and move it up a tone to the sixth note of the scale (so, one white note). You are now playing C Major 6th. Like this:

C Major 6th (C^{M6})

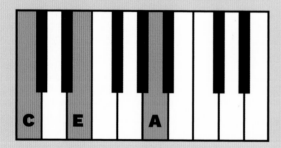

Do exactly the same with F, G, and D. That little finger moves to the sixth, just one note higher than its normal position on the fifth.

F Major

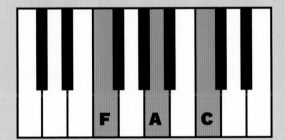 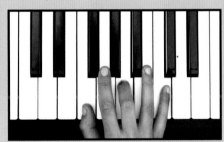

F Major 6th (F^M6)

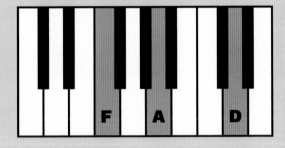 

G Major

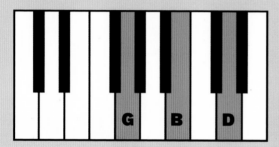

G Major 6th (G^{M6})

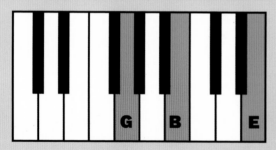

D Major

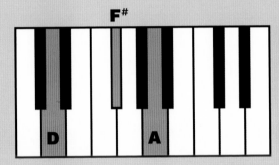 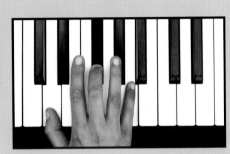

D Major 6th (D^M6)

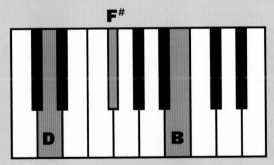 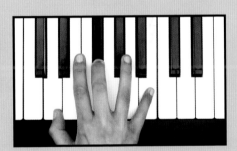

A and E are slightly more complicated, in that traveling a whole tone from the fifth to the sixth takes you from a white note to a black note.

A Major

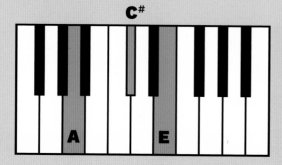
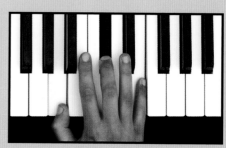

A Major 6th (A^M6^)

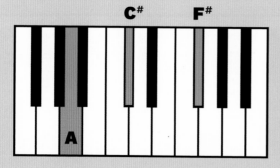

E Major

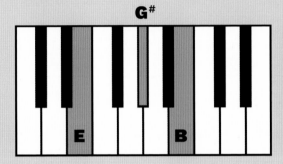

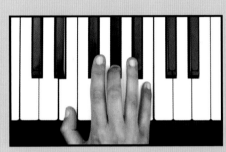

E Major 6th (E^M6^)

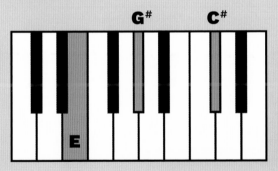

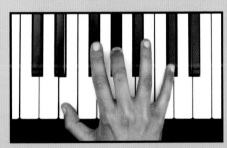

You now know how to play sus 4s, sus 2s, and Major 6ths. Here are a couple of chord sequences that wrap all three chord families together, and work very nicely when played along with a rather groovy song: "Brass in Pocket," by The Pretenders.

CHORD SEQUENCE ONE

Strike the chords on the four beats of the first bar, then take a bar's rest. The left hand plays the root (A) on the first beat of the bar. After eight bars, it changes to F#, though the right hand doesn't change. The sequence ends on D ^{sus2}.

	1	AND	2	AND	3	AND	4	AND		1	AND	2	AND	3	AND	4	AND
Right	A		A		A		A^{sus2}		-								
Left	A								-								

	1	AND	2	AND	3	AND	4	AND		1	AND	2	AND	3	AND	4	AND
Right	A^{sus4}		A^{sus4}		A^{sus4}		A		-								
Left	A								-								

	1	AND	2	AND	3	AND	4	AND		1	AND	2	AND	3	AND	4	AND
Right	A		A		A		A^{sus2}		-								
Left	A								-								

	1	AND	2	AND	3	AND	4	AND		1	AND	2	AND	3	AND	4	AND
Right	A^{sus4}		A^{sus4}		A^{sus4}		A		-								
Left	A								-								

	1	AND	2	AND	3	AND	4	AND		1	AND	2	AND	3	AND	4	AND
Right	A		A		A		A^{sus2}		-								
Left	F#								-								

	1	AND	2	AND	3	AND	4	AND		1	AND	2	AND	3	AND	4	AND
Right	A^{sus4}		A^{sus4}		A^{sus4}		A		-								
Left	F#								-								

	1	AND	2	AND	3	AND	4	AND		1	AND	2	AND	3	AND	4	AND
Right	D^{sus2}		D^{sus2}		D^{sus2}		D^{sus2}		-								
Left	D								-								

	1	AND	2	AND	3	AND	4	AND		1	AND	2	AND	3	AND	4	AND
Right	D^{sus2}		D^{sus2}		D^{sus2}		D^{sus2}		-								
Left	D								-								

Founding member Chrissie Hynde comes from Ohio, but became hooked on the U.K. music scene and de-camped to London, where she worked as a rock journalist. "Brass in pocket" is a northern English phrase for money, which delighted Chrissie enough to write the song, though she then professed to detesting the number. Nevertheless, it went in at number one and earned her plenty of "brass in pocket" of her own!

CHORD SEQUENCE TWO

As Chrissie Hynde goes through her moves, "Gonna use my arms, gonna use my legs," we're going to throw in a few moves of our own: Major 6ths and sus 4s.

	1	AND	2	AND	3	AND	4	AND		1	AND	2	AND	3	AND	4	AND
Right	E^{M6}		E^{M6}		E^{M6}		E		-								
Left	E								-								

	1	AND	2	AND	3	AND	4	AND		1	AND	2	AND	3	AND	4	AND
Right	E^{sus4}		E^{sus4}		E^{sus4}		E		-								
Left	E								-								

	1	AND	2	AND	3	AND	4	AND		1	AND	2	AND	3	AND	4	AND
Right	E^{M6}		E^{M6}		E^{M6}		E		-								
Left	E								-								

	1	AND	2	AND	3	AND	4	AND		1	AND	2	AND	3	AND	4	AND
Right	E^{sus4}		E^{sus4}		E^{sus4}		E		-								
Left	E								-								

MUSICAL NOTATION: COUNTING TIME

You're used to counting yourself in: *one two three four*. Also, the busier count: *one and two and three and four and*. If you'd like to know more . . .

Quarter note or crotchet and rest

One two three four—you are counting in quarter notes here, or in other words, dividing the bar into four. Those quarter notes are also known as crotchets. In musical notation, they look like this:

So, when looking at a formal piece of music, you can recognize this note not only by its pitch—where it sits on the stave—but by its shape and therefore its duration, how long it lasts. Also, in musical notation, it may be that you are required not to play a note, for that duration of time (i.e., for one beat of the bar). There is a symbol for this quarter note rest:

Eighth note or quaver and rest

One and two and three and four and—now you are counting in eighth beats, or quavers. A quaver on its own has a little tail. When two quavers occur one after the other, their tails are replaced with a beam, joining the two together, like this:

When you are *not* required to play for that duration, you will see this symbol:

You begin to see how all those mystifying notes and squiggles against a backdrop of lines might not be so mystical after all. The lines and the spaces between them give us our notes. The shape of those notes tells us how long they last. The shape of the rests tell us how long to wait before the next note. This combination of crotchets, quavers, and rests always adds up to the amount of beats in the bar, in a perfectly calculable way.

PRACTICE WHAT YOU'VE LEARNED

C $^{2nd\ inv}$ – G – A^m – E $^{1st\ inv}$ – F – G – C $^{2nd\ inv}$, A^m, G

Here are a few shapes of chords—a mixture of root and inversions—chosen so that they cluster together as closely as possible, to minimize movement from one to the other.

Before getting to grips with this sequence, a good reference track for you to listen to would be the Oasis song "Don't Look Back in Anger." It will give you a steady tempo and guide you home. Not all the song will work with the sequence, but it perfectly fits the verses and the "So Sally can wait" chorus.

Let's break it down:

C $^{2nd\ inv}$ – G

As you did in the last sequence, move fingers 2 and 5 downward by one white note to change chord.

A^m – E $^{1st\ inv}$

Move finger 1 and finger 2 down a semitone to change chord.

F – G – C $^{2nd\ inv}$

F to G is easy enough—it's the same shape-one chord moving up by one white note. G to C $^{2nd\ inv}$ – move finger 2 and finger 5 up one white note to change chord.

A^m – G

End with these two shape-one chords: A^m moving down one white note to G Major.

Each chord lasts for one bar, until the last two chords (A^m, G), which are two beats each. The tempo is a brisk four beats per bar. Play along with the track to really nail this.

AND THE COMMITTEE RULES—YOU'RE A JOOLS!

There are different stories as to how the song "Don't Look Back in Anger" came about. One is that Noel Gallagher was messing around on stage during a sound check. Brother Liam asked, "Did you just sing 'so Sally can wait?'" He didn't, but Noel liked it, so started singing it, and the song just fell out from there. It pays homage to John Lennon: the intro is similar to the piano intro from "Imagine," and the lyrics "So I start a revolution from my bed" refers to John and Yoko's Amsterdam Hilton "bed-in."

LEVEL FIVE: KEYS

Hip-hop icon Alicia Augello Cook has sold more than 35 million albums. As someone who chose her professional name to represent her piano talent and whose first album, *Songs in A Minor*, names one of the first chords you learned, we simply had to give her name to this level: Alicia Keys. In this final level, we add more chord families to your repertoire, and develop your knowledge and techniques to improve your skills.

MORE CHORD FAMILIES

A Major 7th chord is denoted by a small triangle beside the letter of the chord and it is played—in the root position—by going down a *half step* (one semitone) with finger 1 from the root note of the chord (the first). With the left hand, however, you still play the root note. Here, for example, is the first chord you learned in this book, C Major, played as a Major 7th.

C△

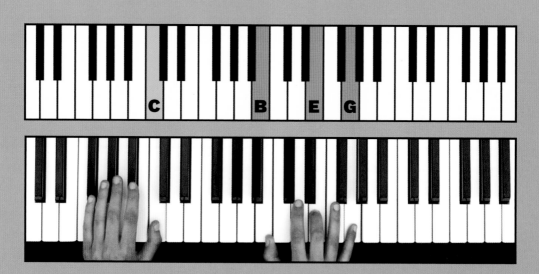

MAJOR 7THS

Here is A, including inversions—the following illustrations show both the left and right hands on the keyboard.

A△

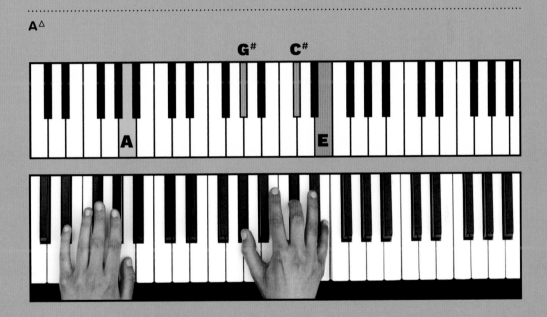

A △ 1st inv

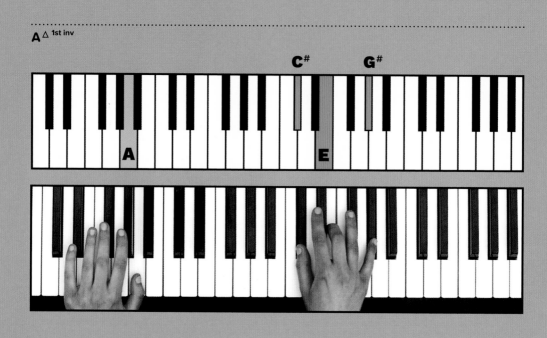

A △ 2nd inv

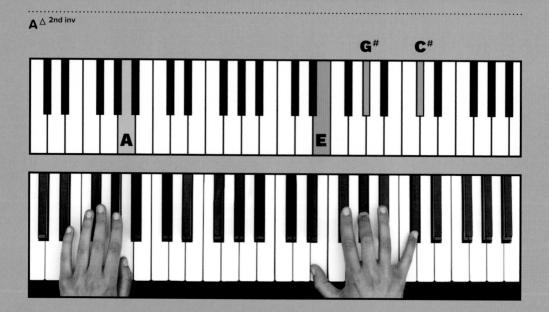

And now here are B to G, including inversions—the following illustrations show only the right hand on the keyboard. Remember, the left hand plays the root note of the chord.

B△

A#   D#   F#

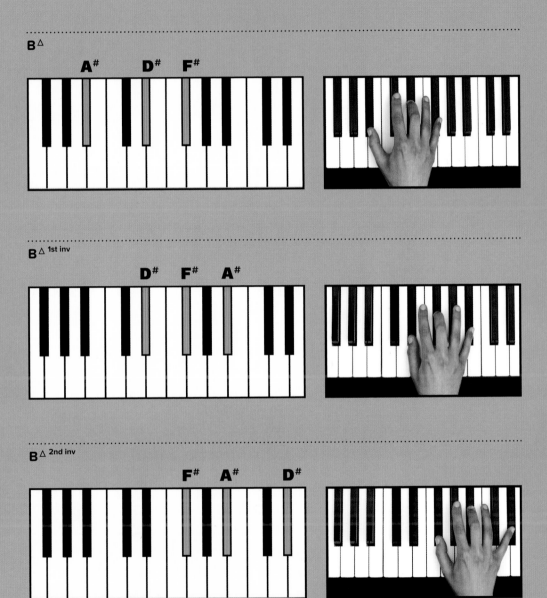

B△ 1st inv

D#   F#   A#

B△ 2nd inv

F#   A#   D#

C△

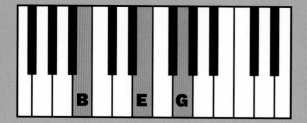
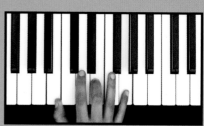

C△ 1st inv

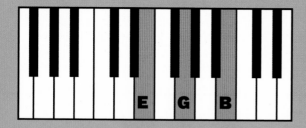

C△ 2nd inv

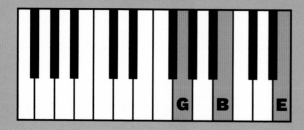

D△

C#   **F**#

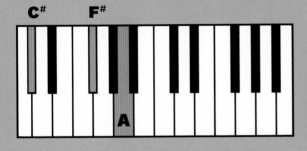

A

D△ **1st inv**

F#   **C**#

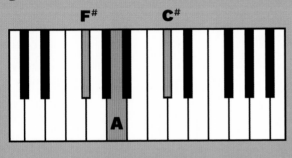

A

D△ **2nd inv**

C#   **F**#

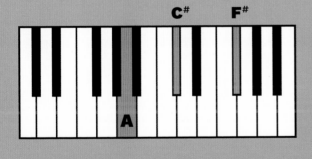

A

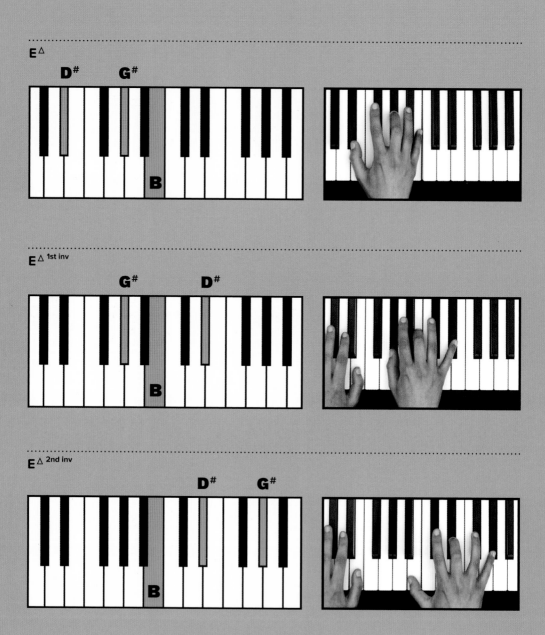

E△

D# G#

B

E△ 1st inv

G# D#

B

E△ 2nd inv

D# G#

B

F△

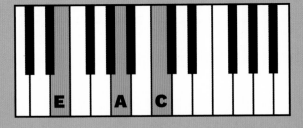 

F△ 1st inv

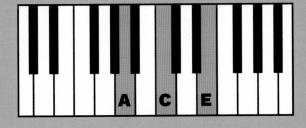 

F△ 2nd inv

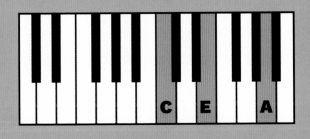 

G△

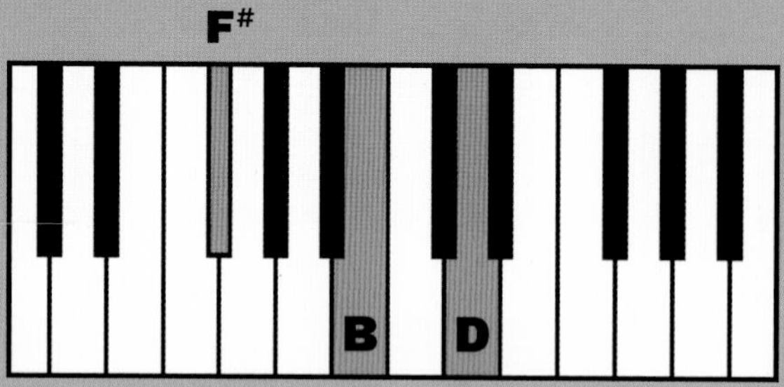

F#

B D

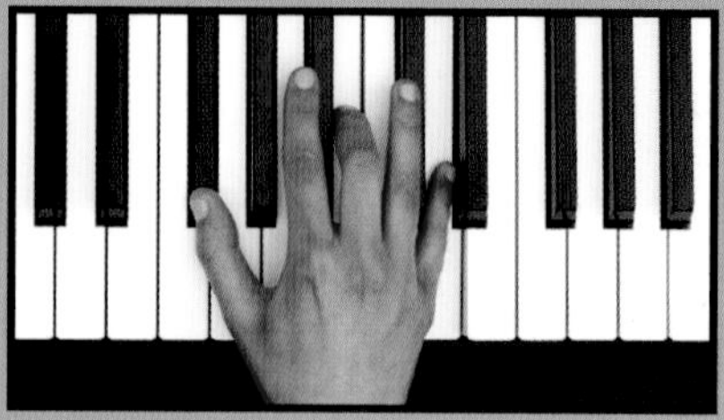

G△ 1st inv

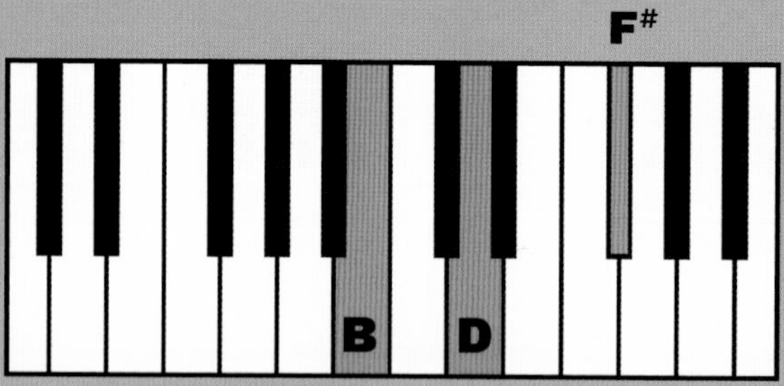

F#

B D

G△ 2nd inv

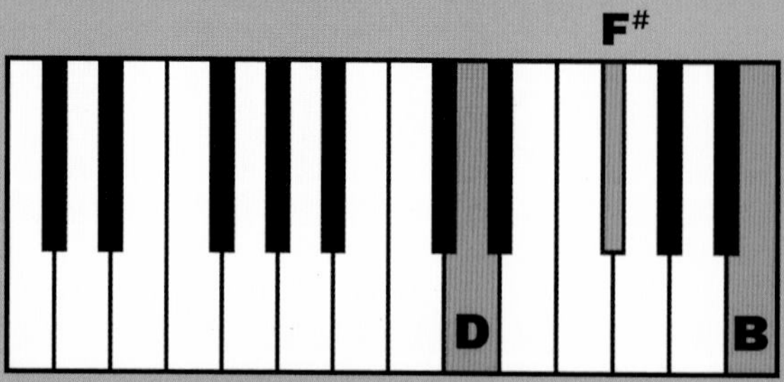

F#

D B

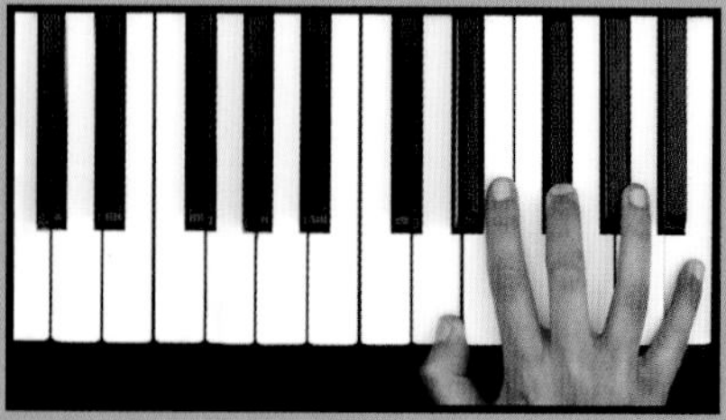

DOMINANT 7TH

Dominant 7th is the fancy name—that really isn't how we refer to them; they're 7ths. They are absolute staple pop chords. But by calling them dominant 7ths for now helps distinguish them from the Major 7ths you've just encountered. They sound radically different; don't get confused between the two. These are poppy 7ths; the others are jazzy Major 7ths.

With the Major 7ths, you went down a half step (semitone) from the root note of the chord—the first.

With these, you go down a *whole step* (two semitones) from the first note. Meanwhile, the left hand still plays the root note of the chord.

The following illustrations show both the left and right hands on the keyboard playing A⁷ᵗʰ with its inversions.

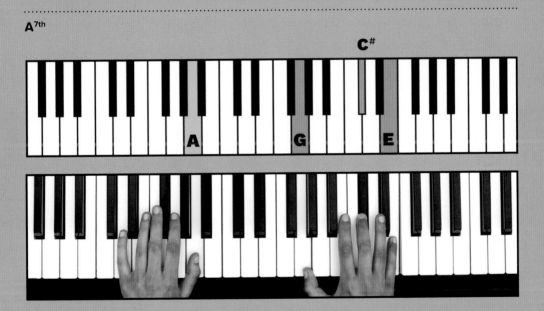

A⁷ᵗʰ

A7th 1st inv

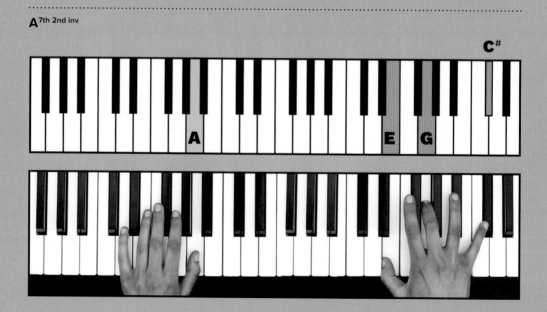

A7th 2nd inv

And now here are B⁷ᵗʰ to G⁷ᵗʰ, including inversions—the following illustrations show only the right hand on the keyboard. Remember, the left hand stills plays the root note of the chord.

B⁷ᵗʰ

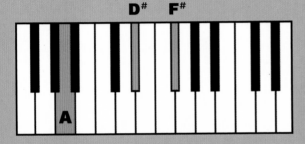 

B⁷ᵗʰ 1st inv

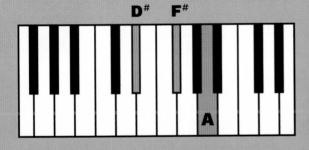 

B⁷ᵗʰ 2nd inv

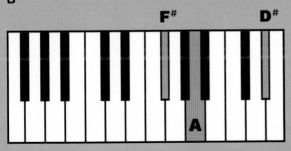 

C⁷th

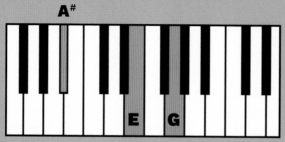

C⁷th 1st inv

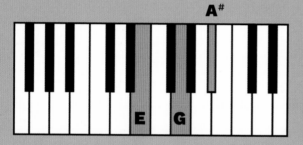

C⁷th 2nd inv

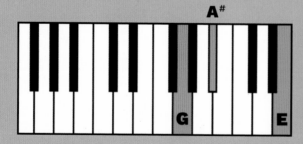

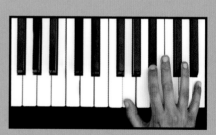

D^{7th}

F#

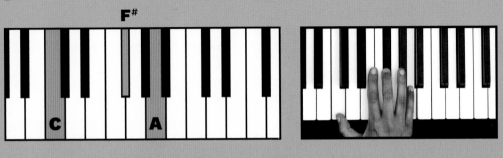

C   A

D^{7th 1st inv}

F#

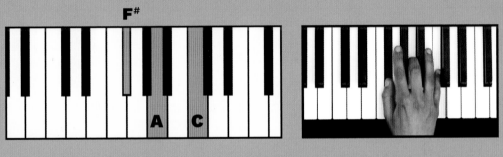

A   C

D^{7th 2nd inv}

F#

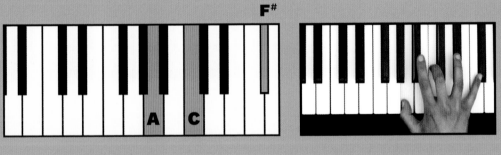

A   C

E^{7th}

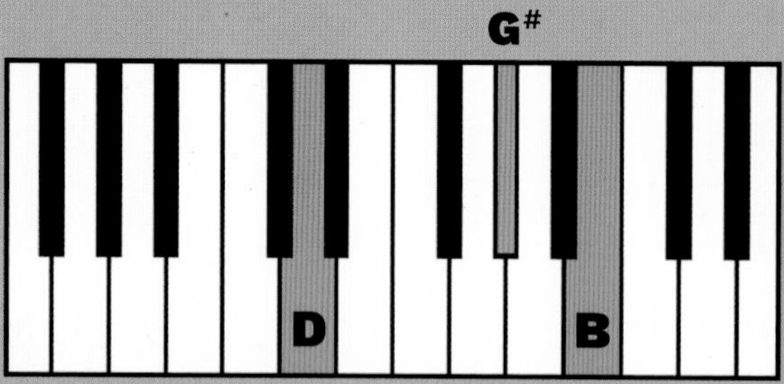

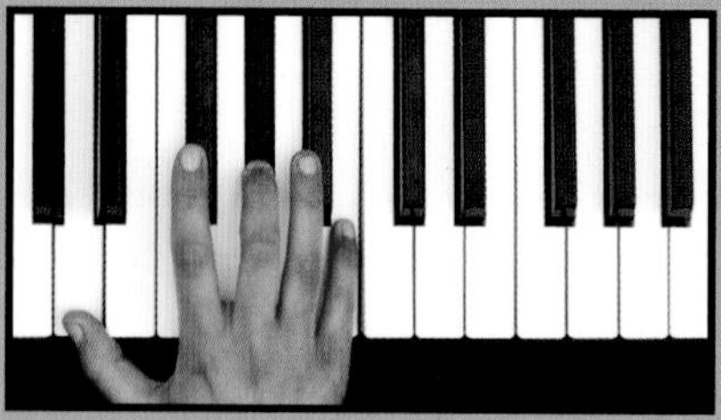

E^{7th 1st inv}

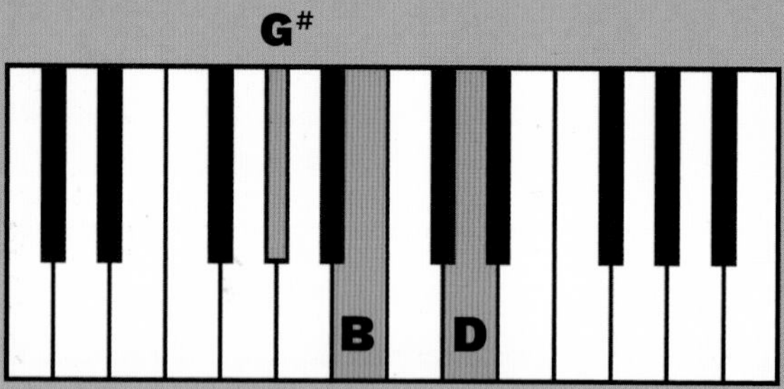

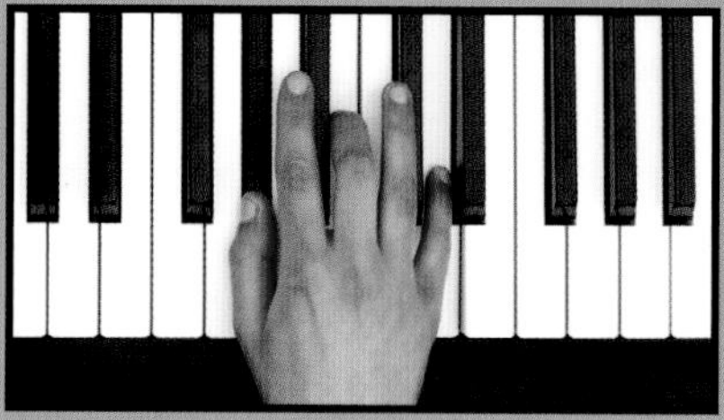

E^{7th 2nd inv}

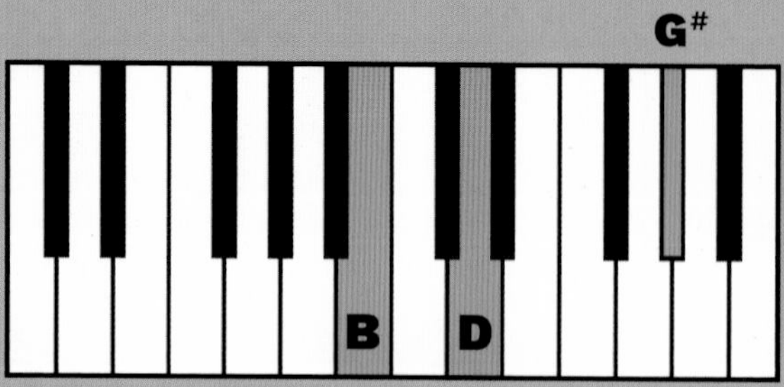

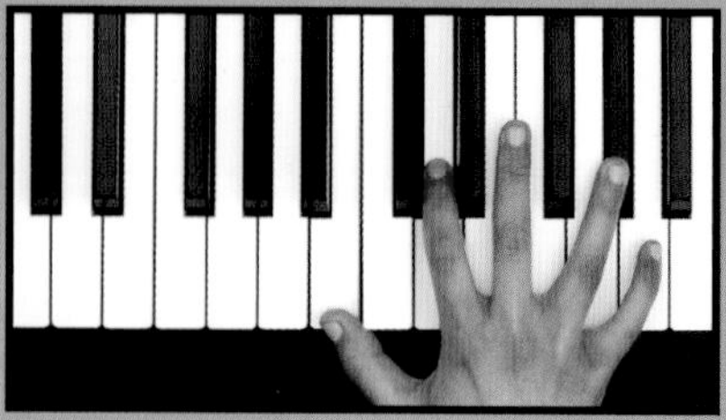

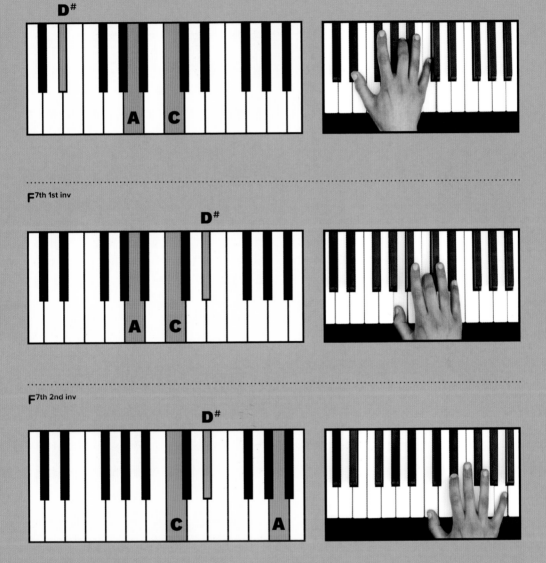

F7th

F7th 1st inv

F7th 2nd inv

G^{7th}

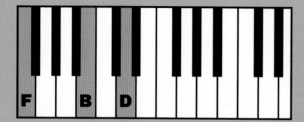 

G^{7th 1st inv}

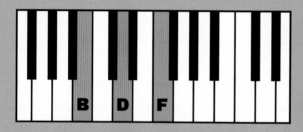 

G^{7th 2nd inv}

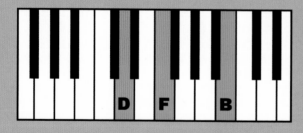 

Phew—time out, let's have a number! And let's make it one whose DNA is shot through with the chord you've just learned, the dominant 7th.

Here's the sequence: it has gentle shape-one root chords all the way, with a couple of big 7ths thrown in. Just move finger 1 down one tone from the chord before and you've got it.

We're in the friendly key of C, slow count of four, one-in-the-bar. Easy! The left hand plays the root note on every chord but one (bar five—there's always one, isn't there?). Also, watch out for a pretty hectic penultimate bar where you play a different chord on every beat.

	1	2	3	4		1	2	3	4
Right	C				-	C⁷			
Left	C				-	C			

	1	2	3	4		1	2	3	4
Right	F				-	D			
Left	F				-	D			

	1	2	3	4		1	2	3	4
Right	C				-	G			
Left	G				-	G			

	1	2	3	4		1	2	3	4
Right	C				-	C⁷			
Left	C				-	C			

	1	2	3	4		1	2	3	4
Right	F				-	Dm	Em	F	G
Left	F				-	D	E	F	G

	1	2	3	4		1	2	3	4
Right	C				-				
Left	C				-				

This fits very nicely with the chorus of "Don't Let the Sun Go Down on Me."

"Don't Let the Sun Go Down on Me" was written by Elton John and lyricist Bernie Taupin with the aim of it being an epic production in the style of Phil Spector's "You've Lost That Lovin' Feelin'." It was also influenced by The Beach Boys—two of whom sang the harmonies. Seventeen years later, Elton and his friend George Michael recorded it as a duet and it went to number one on both sides of the Atlantic.

MINOR 7THS

You can easily find minor 7ths, now that you know how to play dominant 7ths. Simply apply the same formula to a minor chord instead of a Major chord. Here's the chord after which Alicia named her first album: A minor. While still playing the root note with the left hand, move finger 1 from the root played by the right hand down a whole step (two semitones).

A MINOR 7TH

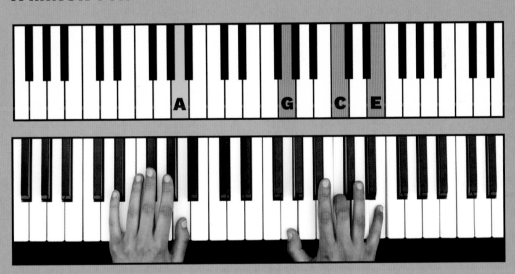

That's one way of doing it. However, we're going to approach this slightly differently, by *adding* the 7th at the *top* of the chord. For the first time, you will be playing a *four-note chord* instead of a triad. To do so will involve four fingers: fingers 1, 2, 3, and 5—or use fingers 1, 2, 4, and 5 if you find this more comfortable.

Here's how you do it:

- Play a normal (root version) **A**ᵐ.

- As you would do if you were looking for the first inversion, visually locate the root note (A) one octave higher. Don't play it, just locate that high A.

- From there, go down a whole step (two semitones) to the G. This is the 7th, the note we're going to add.

Aᵐ⁷

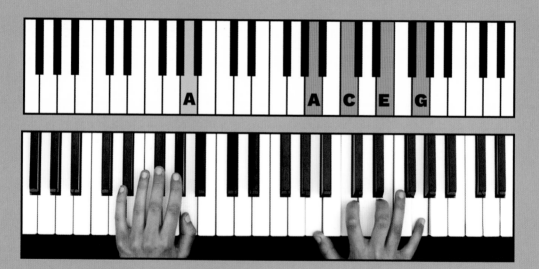

Now have a go at repositioning the chord in the usual way we do with inversions, by playing the lowest note an octave higher instead. Because you are playing four notes now, there is one more position than usual before we find ourselves back in the first position, an octave up.

Am7 2nd position

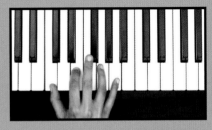

Am7 3rd position

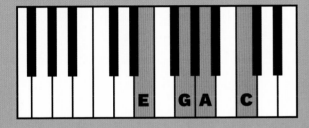

Am7 4th position

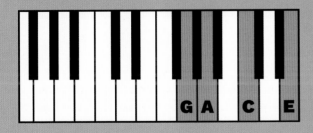

Here are B, C, D, E, F, and G. Once you have mastered these, try finding your own minor 7ths on A#, C#, D#, F#, and G#, in all four positions.

B MINOR 7TH

B^{m7} 1st position

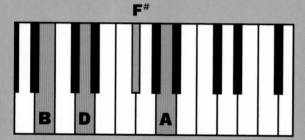

B^{m7} 2nd position

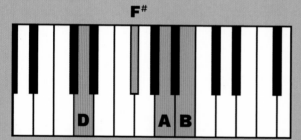

Bm7 **3rd position**

F#

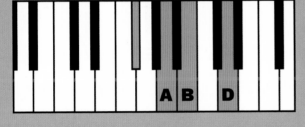

A B D

Bm7 **4th position**

F#

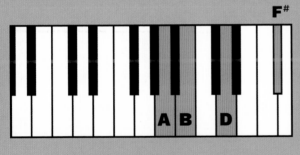

A B D

C MINOR 7TH

C^m7 1st position

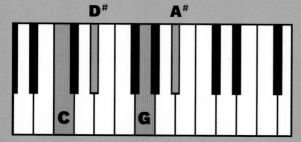

C^m7 2nd position

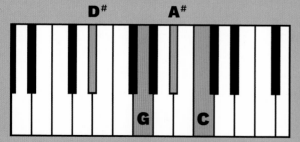

C^{m7} 3rd position

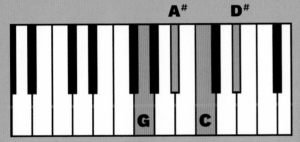

C^{m7} 4th position

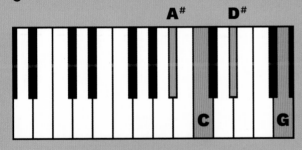

D MINOR 7TH

Dm7 1st position

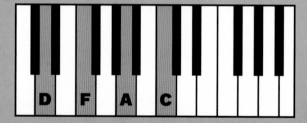

Dm7 2nd position

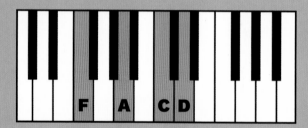

Dm7 3rd position

Dm7 4th position

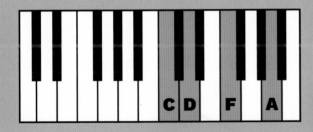 

E MINOR 7TH

Em7 1st position

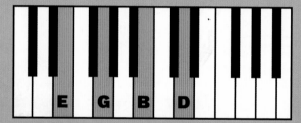 

Em7 2nd position

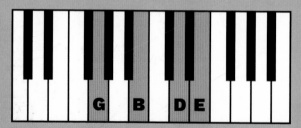 

Em7 3rd position

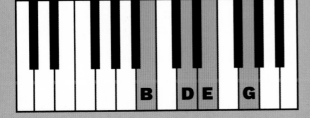

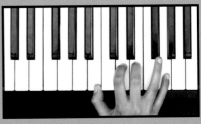

Em7 4th position

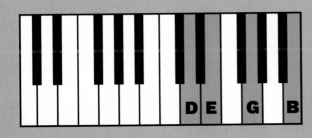

F MINOR 7TH

Fm7 1st position

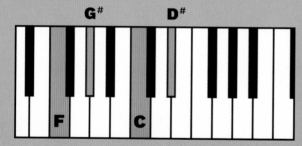

Fm7 2nd position

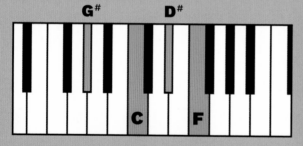

Fm7 3rd position

D#   G#

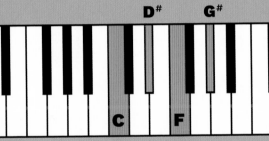

C   F

Fm7 4th position

D#   G#

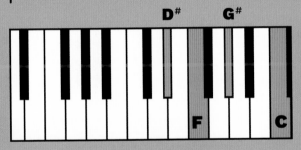

F   C

G MINOR 7TH

Gm7 1st position

A#

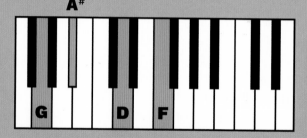

G   **D**   **F**

Gm7 2nd position

A#

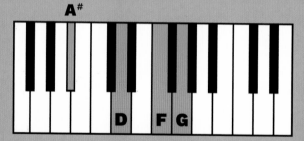

D   **F** **G**

Gm7 3rd position

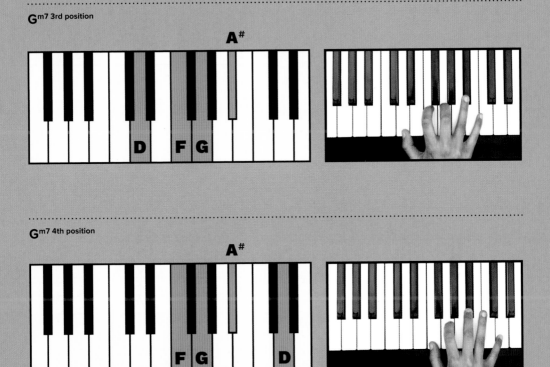

Gm7 4th position

6/8 TIME SIGNATURE

We have been using a 4/4 time signature exclusively so far. But there are others. And what do those two numbers actually mean?

- The top number refers to the number of beats in the bar.

- The lower number refers to the *type* of notes we are measuring by—quarter notes, eighth notes, etc.

For now, let's just concentrate on the top figure. We've been counting four beats, but now we are going to count six beats in the bar, as we switch to a 6/8 time signature. Every rhythm, every song, has a pulse, a groove. When you count it in six, put the emphasis on the one and the four, like this: **one** two three **four** five six.

CHORD SEQUENCE: $E^{m\ 2nd\ inv} - B^{m7} - E^{m\ 1st\ inv} - B^{m7}$

Here's a four-chord, four-bar sequence for you, one chord per bar, which will be played on the first beat of each of the six-beat measures (a measure is another word for a bar).

There are only two chords: E^m and B^{m7}, but we are doing different inversions of each of those chords in bars three and four. It is presented to you here in a slightly different form, with the notes written one on top of the other.

1	2	3	4	5	6	1	2	3	4	5	6	1	2	3	4	5	6	1	2	3	4	5	6
G						F#						E						D					
E						D						B						A					
B						A						G						F#					

The left hand, meanwhile, is just playing the root: E with the first chord, B with the second, E with the third chord, and B with the fourth.

Instead of striking the chord, you are going to arpeggiate it, one note on each of the six beats of the bar. This time, the left-hand note will fall on the first beat of the bar. The right hand plays up through the chord on beats two, three, and four, then back down through the chord on beats five and six. Like this:

	1	2	3	4	5	6		1	2	3	4	5	6
Right		B	E	G	E	B	-		A	D	F#	D	A
Left	E						-	B					

	1	2	3	4	5	6		1	2	3	4	5	6
Right		G	B	E	B	G	-		F#	A	D	A	F#
Left	E						-	B					

I'll bet you didn't know you were playing Chopin just now! But you actually were. Alicia Keys referred to Chopin as "my dawg" and built her smash hit "Fallin'" upon a piece of his music.

CIRCLE OF FIFTHS

Here, all the information you have absorbed over the course of this book comes together in one perfect diagram . . .

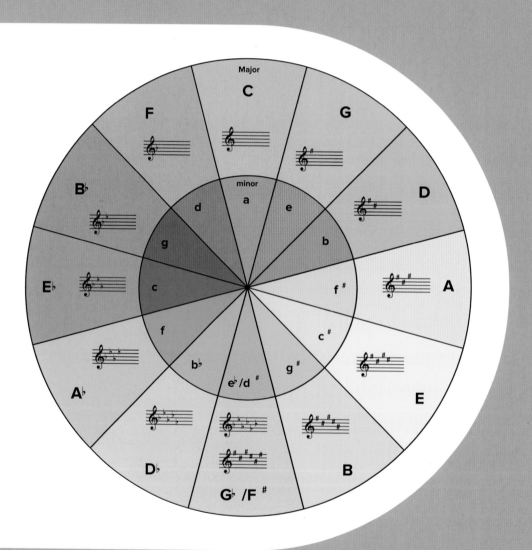

UNDERSTANDING THIS DIAGRAM

The mystical wheel pictured here is known as the circle of fifths. Everything you've read about in this book about scales, firsts, fourths, and fifths, Major chords, and relative minors is all here, at a glance, in this diagram.

What the uppercase letters mean

The bold capital letters around the outside are the various keys, placed clockwise in fifths. Counterclockwise, they are a fourth apart. This is handy. The three primary Majors you need for any given key are the first, the fourth, and the fifth, right? The first is the bold capital letter. The fourth is on its left and the fifth on its right. C for instance has F (the fourth) and G (fifth) to its left and right. G has C and D to either side of it. And so on, all the way around.

Sharps and flats

Each segment contains the number of sharps or flats associated with that key, too. At the top, in the 12 o'clock position, stands C, which has no sharps or flats. As we read around the circle traveling clockwise, a sharp is added to each segment until we hit 6 o'clock. Then they turn to flats, traveling up and around the left-hand side of the diagram, decreasing by one flat each segment, until we arrive back at C at the top.

What the lowercase letters mean

Furthermore, if you look at the inner circle with its lowercase letters, you will see that these are the relevant minors pertaining to each of the Major keys above them. It's beautifully neat. At a glance, you have all the information you need. Pick any key—A, say. What are the primary Majors? D to the left, E to the right. What is the number of black notes in the scale? Three. The relative minor? F#.

You can always refer to this diagram for all the information you need.

ROCKING YOUR CHORD

Here is one last number. You know how to put all three notes down together and strike a chord. You know how to play each note in sequence and arpeggiate a chord. But, there is a third way. While your left hand continues to play the root note of each chord in the usual way, your right hand is going to be "rocking" your chord backward and forward.

Look at the first two chords in this eight-bar sequence: F Major 2nd inversion and good old ordinary C Major—finger 1, finger 3, and finger 5 on the three notes from left to right.

Your head needs to be counting *one and two and three and four and* as your two fingers play their two notes together on each counted number as it comes along. Finger 1 plays on each of the "ands" in between. Like this:

1	AND	2	AND	3	AND	4	AND		1	AND	2	AND	3	AND	4	AND
A		A		A		A		-	G		G		G		G	
F		F		F		F		-	E		E		E		E	
	C		C		C		C			C		C		C		C

For the next two bars, stay on the C for bar three and go back to the F $^{2nd\ inv}$ for bar four:

1	AND	2	AND	3	AND	4	AND		1	AND	2	AND	3	AND	4	AND
G		G		G		G		-	A		A		A		A	
E		E		E		E		-	F		F		F		F	
	C		C		C		C			C		C		C		C

B^b $^{1st\ inv}$ in bar five, going back to the F on bar six:

1	AND	2	AND	3	AND	4	AND		1	AND	2	AND	3	AND	4	AND
B♭		B♭		B♭		B♭		-	A		A		A		A	
F		F		F		F		-	F		F		F		F	
	D		D		D		D			C		C		C		C

Bars seven and eight are exactly the same as three and four, i.e., C chord back to F chord:

1	AND	2	AND	3	AND	4	AND		1	AND	2	AND	3	AND	4	AND
G		G		G		G		-	A		A		A		A	
E		E		E		E		-	F		F		F		F	
	C		C		C		C			C		C		C		C

By Jove—or should I say, "Hey Jude"—you've done well. The "*na na na*" bit at the end goes F to E flat to B flat and back to F, but you can work it out for yourself, any inversion you like, because not only are you now a Keys, you're a keyboard player, too!

THIS BOOK DECREES: YOU'RE A KEYS!

GLOSSARY

arpeggiate—Play each individual note of a chord, in a sequence.

augmented—A chord that contains intervals that are one semitone higher than the corresponding Major.

bar—A short measure of music.

bass clef stave—Represents the keys below middle C on your keyboard.

beat—A unit of musical rhythm.

blues—A type of music of African-American folk origin, usually in a twelve-bar sequence.

bridge—The part of a song that gives you a change from the repetition of the verse and chorus.

chord—A group of notes played together.

chorus—A repetitious part of a song designed to make you remember it.

crotchet—A single beat note, or a quarter of a four-beat bar. Also called a quarter note.

diminished—A chord with its intervals as the first, flat third, and flat fifth of the Major scale.

dominant 7th—A type of chord that is used to expand or make another chord sound like the home key.

eighth note—An eighth of a bar in 4/4 time. Also called a quaver.

electric keyboard—An electronic musical instrument with keys set out as on a piano.

flat—A symbol that indicates a note is to be lowered by one semitone.

grand piano—A large musical instrument made up of the body with three legs, strings, soundboard, and keys.

half step—The shortest interval you can travel on a keyboard, between two adjacent notes. Also called a semitone.

interval—The distance between two notes.

inversion—The act of turning a chord into three chords, using a simple formula, allowing you to play a chord in a variety of positions.

key—A group of notes based on and named after a particular note and comprising a scale.

ledger line—A short line running through the note in question.

Major chord—A chord with its intervals at the first, third, and fifth notes of the Major scale.

measure—Another name for a bar.

minor chord—A chord with its intervals as the first, flat third, and fifth notes of the Major scale.

musical notation—A language; a series of written symbols on the stave, used to represent the pitch and duration of musical notes and the length of silences between them.

musical stave (*see* stave)

note—A single tone of a fixed pitch.

octave—A series of eight notes from the root note to when the root note next occurs on the keyboard.

pedal—There are several different types of pedal: old-fashioned acoustic pianos usually have two: the left is a soft pedal, which softens the sound when pressed; the right is a sustain pedal, which keeps the note ringing when pressed. Modern and grand pianos tend to have three pedals: the third is a "damper," which stops the note ringing when pressed. All are operated by the feet.

pentatonic scale—A scale of five notes.

pitch—The wave frequency of a note.

play by ear—The ability to play music without needing to read musical notation.

primary Majors—The three chords associated with a particular key that are built upon the first, fourth, and fifth notes of the scale.

quarter note—A single beat note, or a quarter of a four-beat bar. Also called a crotchet.

quaver—An eighth of a bar in 4/4 time. Also called an eighth note.

relative minor—The scale starting three semitones below its relative major, and containing the same notes.

resolve—A chord that provides a resolution to the suspended chord before it.

root—The first note of a scale or chord. Also called a tonic.

scale—A series of notes in ascending or descending order of pitch that lie within an octave.

semitone—The shortest interval you can travel on a keyboard, between two adjacent notes. Also called a half step.

sequence—An arranged succession of chords or notes to be played.

sequence of intervals—Every major scale played has this sequence of intervals: 2 2 1 2 2 2 1

sharp—A symbol to indicate a note is to be raised by one semitone.

stave—A set of five horizontal lines with spaces between them on which musical notes are written to show their pitch.

sus/suspended—A dominant chord where a note is replaced by the next note, a half step higher.

tempo—The speed at which music is played.

time signature—This appears at the beginning of a piece of music and indicates the rhythm of a piece. The top figure represents the number of beats in the bar. The lower figure represents the type of beat by which the bar is measured.

tone—This is equal to two semitones. It is also a sound characterized by its pitch, quality, and strength.

tonic—The first note of a scale or chord. Also called a root.

treble clef stave—Represents the notes above middle C on your keyboard.

triad—Another name for a chord, but it must contain three notes.

verse—A group of words that form a unit in a song.

INDEX

A (the note of) 9
A dominant 7th 145–6
A flat 32
A Major 47, 83, 126
    inversions 50–1
    Major 6th 126
    Major 7th 137–8
    root 49
    scale 97
A minor 21, 31
    inversions 40–1
    minor 7th 155–7
A sharp Major 59, 83, 87
    inversions 62
    root 62
A sharp minor 78
A suspended fourth 105
A suspended second 114
arpeggiating 25–6, 28, 55, 61, 171, 174
augmented chords 104

B (the note of) 9
B dominant 7th 147
B flat 32, 34
B Major 60
    inversions 63
    Major 7th 139
    root 63
    scale 99
B minor 79
    minor 7th 158–9
B suspended fourth 106
B suspended second 114
Bach 101
bars 24
bass clef stave 45
Beach Boys 154
Berlin, Irving 70–1
black notes 9, 26, 31, 32, 46, 54, 71, 173
Blues 30
Bowie, David 64–7
bridge 33
Brooker, Gary 101

C (the note of) 9
C dominant 7th 148
C Major 11, 18, 26–8, 30, 122
    converting to minor 72
    double scale 45
    inversions 38–41
    Major 6th 122
    Major 7th 136, 140
    primary chords 30

relative minor 31
    scale 25–7
    six-chord trick 31–2
C minor 72, 74
    minor 7th 160–1
C sharp Major 54
    inversions 56
    root 56
C sharp minor 76
C suspended fourth 107
C suspended second 115
Carmichael, Hoagy 29
Chopin 170–1
chord families 10, 104, 122, 127, 136
chord shapes 10–11, 46
    shape one 18, 19, 24, 28, 33, 64, 92
    shape two 47–51, 92
    shape three 54–8
    shape four 74–5
    shape five 76–7
    Random (R) shapes 59–63, 64, 78–9
circle of fifths 172–3
Cocker, Joe 43
Cohen, Leonard 30
crotchet 68, 131, 132

D (the note of) 9
D dominant 7th 149
D flat 32
D Major 47, 125
    inversions 52
    Major 6th 125
    Major 7th 141
    root 52
    scale 96
D minor 19, 31, 82
    minor 7th 162–3
D sharp Major 54
    inversions 57
    root 57
D sharp minor 78, 86
D suspended fourth 107
D suspended second 115
damper pedal 13
diminished chords 104
dominant 7ths 104, 145–53

E (the note of) 9
E dominant 7th 150
E flat 32
E Major 48, 127
    inversions 53
    Major 6th 127

    Major 7th 142
    root 53
    scale 98
E minor 19, 31
    minor 7th 164–5
E suspended fourth 108
E suspended second 116
eighth beats 68–9, 131
eighth note 131
electronic keyboards 12, 13

F (the note of) 9
F dominant 7th 151
F Major 20, 30, 31, 123
    converting to minor 73
    Major 6th 123
    Major 7th 143
    primary majors 94
    relative minor chord 31
    relative minors 94
    scale 93–4
F minor 73, 74
    minor 7th 166–7
F sharp Major 59
    inversions 61
    root 61
F sharp minor 76
F suspended fourth 108
F suspended second 116
fifths 28, 30
fingers 12
first inversion 38–41
Fisher, Matthew 101
flats 9, 32–3, 46, 95
fourths 28, 30

G (the note of) 9
G dominant 7th 152
G flat 32
G Major 20, 30, 124
    Major 6th 124
    Major 7th 144
    primary majors 92
    relative minor chord 31
    relative minors 92
    scale 90–2
G minor 75, 82
    minor 7th 168–9
G sharp Major 55
    inversions 58
    root 58
G sharp minor 77, 86
G suspended fourth 109

G suspended second 117
Green, Al 22
Gallagher, Liam 133
Gallagher, Noel 133

half step 8, 136
hand positioning 14
Hanks, Tom 29
Hawkins, Jay 80–1
Holland, Jools 102–3
Hynde, Chrissie 128–30

intervals 27–8, 95
inversions 38–41
    combining 64
    shape two 49–53
    shape three 55–8
    shape R 61–3

John, Elton 7, 153–4
Jones, Tom 22

Keys, Alicia 134–5, 155, 171
King, B.B. 103
Kings of Leon 42–3
Koch, Martin 7

Lady Gaga 36–7, 69
ledger lines 44
left hand 12, 40–2, 100
    root note 51
Lennon, John 35, 133
lines and spaces 44–5
Lott, Pixie 88–9

McCartney, Paul 16–17, 35
Major 6ths 122–30
Major 7ths 104, 136–44
Major chords 30, 104
    converting to minor 72–3
    root chords 64
Major/minor chords
    mix one 82–4
    mix two 86–8
Mars, Bruno 110–11
Michael, George 154
middle C 18, 44–5
minor 7ths 155–69
minor chords 104
    converting from Major 72–3
    relative minors 31, 88
    root chords 80

musical notation 24, 44–5, 131–2
Oasis 132–3
octaves 9, 27

pedals 13
pitch 9, 131
Presley, Elvis 72, 73, 111
primary Major chords 30, 88
Procul Harum 101

quarter beats 24–5, 68
quarter note 131
quaver 68, 131

relative minor chords 31, 88, 92
resolve 105–7
rests 131
right hand 10, 12, 100
Ronson, Mark 85
root chords 64
root note 41, 48, 49, 51
root position 38
Rotten, Johnny 129

scales
    C Major 25–7
    double 45
    intervals 27–8
    major 27
    six-chord trick 31–2
    three-chord trick 30
second inversion 38–41
semitone 8, 9, 27, 31
sharps 9, 46, 95
Simone, Nina 81
six-chord trick 31–2
Sledge, Percy 101
soft pedal 13
Spector, Phil 154
staves 44–5
stickers 7, 10–11
suspended fourths 104, 105–13, 117–21
suspended seconds 104, 114–21
sustain pedal 13

Taupin, Bernie 153–4
The Beatles 6, 34, 35, 174–5
thirds 28
three-chord trick 30
thumbs 12
time 24
    4/4 eighth beats 68–9

4/4 quarter beats 24–5, 68
6/8 170
    eight beats in the bar 69
    four beats in the bar 68
    musical notation 131–2
    three beats in the bar 48
time signature 24
    6/8 170
tone 8
tonic 38
treble clef stave 44–5
triads 31, 104
Turner, Tina 22

Warnes, Jennifer 43
whole step 8
Winehouse, Amy 84–5
Withers, Bill 22–3
Wonder, Stevie 22
wrists 14

Acknowledgments

www.rokskool.co.uk

Rok Skool Sussex gave me the perfect platform for this book. I credit every keyboard student of every age and ability who has sat in front of me these past ten years, and every band I have musically mentored within the Rok Skool environment. Each in their own way showed me what they needed to learn and helped streamline my own method of communication and delivery.

My mission has always been to get people playing by ear as quickly as possible. Rok Skool allowed me to organically develop, then sharpen and hone, the musical approach and systems that I have set down in *Piano Chords: A Keyboard Sticker Book*.

Hereward Kaye

www.herewardkaye.co.uk

Quintet would like to thank Ian Radcliffe from Brighton-based band Shine On for his help on this book.

Credits

Alamy: Michael Brito 16–17; Pictorial Press Ltd 22, 29; AF archive 35; ZUMA Press, Inc. 70–1; Philippe Gras 81; MY – Music 85; imageBROKER 89; dpa picture alliance archive 101; martin phelps 102–3; Newscom 111; Olivier Parent 129; S.I.N. 133; MARKA 134–5; Adam Beeson 154

Getty: Christopher Polk 36–7; David Warner Ellis 65

Shutterstock: Novitech 12; Photosampler 13 (left); yanathep aromoon 13 (right); JStone 43

Neal Grundy (photographer), Hereward Kaye: 6; Melissa Harrison (model): 5, 7, 11, 14–5, 19–21, 25, 34, 40–1, 47–63, 66–7, 72–9, 82–3, 86–7, 90–1, 93, 105–9, 122–7, 136–52, 155–69

+SUBTRACT: piano key illustrations